A HEARTBEAT AWAY

Praises for *A Heartbeat Away*

Your style is so truthful and loving as you explain what you have to say. I just loved the real feelings and love you have for what you were writing about. I think this book will help a lot of people, I really do. I enjoyed your way a explaining things from your heart in such a friendly and loving way. From the verses in the Bible, to the many quotes from people, life examples, and including God in the center of it all. A heartbeat away from Jesus indeed.

I loved the personal experiences which you were blessed enough and smart enough to learn from. As we get older we learn so much from our choice of religion, and from friends. This book is a gentle, honest, and healing walk. The love of which you teach is easily understood and taken to heart. As we get older we understand death more and more, if we are lucky. I think your book will help a great deal of people. People of all ages too, because death has no train schedule for that last ride.

You know your Bible well, Arsen, and this book is going to help many people. Easy to read, written from the heart with great suggestions and inspirations. Sure proud of you my longtime friend. Congratulations and God bless you.

—**Chris Terrence**, Author, Award Winning
TV personality and sports announcer

I just reread your book for content and WOW! It's very compelling! The stories you told are touching, painful, and will grab the reader. (They grabbed my heart!)

You have done a great job with this book. It is concise, gripping, motivational, and informative to the reader. Your message is spot on and we all need to realize we are only "A Heartbeat Away!" It's really the only way we should be living our lives.

—**Richard Smith**, Corporate Executive, Author of,
God versus The Rest of Us

A
HEARTBEAT
AWAY

Are YOU Ready?

ARSEN S. MARSOOBIAN

NASHVILLE

NEW YORK • MELBOURNE • VANCOUVER

A HEARTBEAT AWAY
Are YOU Ready?

Published in New York, New York, by Morgan James Publishing. Morgan James is a trademark of Morgan James, LLC. www.MorganJamesPublishing.com

The Morgan James Speakers Group can bring authors to your live event. For more information or to book an event visit The Morgan James Speakers Group at www.TheMorganJamesSpeakersGroup.com.

Unless otherwise indicated, all scripture quotations in this book are taken from THE HOLY BIBLE, NEW INTERNATIONAL VERSION, LIFE APPLICATION STUDY BIBLE, COPYRIGHT BY TYNDALE HOUSE PUBLISHERS, INC, 1988-1989 1990-1991-2005 PUBLISHED BY ZONDERVAN

ISBN 978-1-68350-641-6 paperback
ISBN 978-1-68350-642-3 eBook
Library of Congress Control Number: 2017909809

Editing assistance by: Performance Publishing Group Plano, TX

Development assistance and formatting by: Robert Mano, author and owner of Mano Y Mano Consulting

Marketing Assistance by: Eric Hughes, Co-Founder of Baby Boomers Community Groups

Cover Design by:
Rachel Lopez
www.r2cdesign.com

Interior Design by:
Bonnie Bushman
The Whole Caboodle Graphic Design

In an effort to support local communities, raise awareness and funds, Morgan James Publishing donates a percentage of all book sales for the life of each book to Habitat for Humanity Peninsula and Greater Williamsburg.

Get involved today! Visit
www.MorganJamesBuilds.com

DEDICATION

The writing of this book, *A Heartbeat Away: Are You Ready?* is being dedicated to a dear friend and in-law, Rosellen Kershaw.

As I am writing this, Rosellen Kershaw is lying in a hospital bed unable to speak, hear, or see clearly. She suffered a stroke nine years ago and a second one four days ago. She was a woman who loved to read and serve more than anyone I've ever met. From the time she had her first stroke nine years ago until the day of the last one, she read a book a day. Rosellen would have been ninety-two this week.

On a personal note, she was extremely influential and helpful in reading manuscripts and making comments for my first book, *Don't Die: 3 Essential Truths for Your Fulfilled and Happy Life*. We talked about this book and what it would cover;

however, she never read any of the drafts, so sadly I missed her reviews. Yet in a strange way, over the last few days she has given me insight into the dying process—insights that will be helpful to me in writing and finishing this book.

Rosellen Kershaw was no ordinary woman. She was the mother of one daughter, Julie Kershaw Marsoobian, my lovely daughter-in-law. She was a crusader, community activist, and a thinker. She adored the community of Fresno. The residents of the city and county of Fresno have much better lives because Rosellen Kershaw lived. For example, we have a phenomenal library system here in City and County of Fresno because she assisted in writing the bond measure and then fought for it to be adopted. In addition, she spearheaded the campaign to bring public radio to our community. Without the funds to hire an executive director, she stepped in as the interim executive director and took no pay for three years, when there were finally enough funds to hire one.

She raised hundreds of thousands of dollars and gave much of her own wealth to causes she believed in. One such cause was the California Armenian Home in Fresno, California, where she has been a resident for the last nine years.

Her love of books and her belief that everyone should have the opportunity to read led her to start a thrift bookstore so people had access to affordable books. She would drive wherever she had to and pick up books donated to the store.

Rosellen served as the head of the League of Women Voters, and was herself extremely active in civic government affairs throughout the 60s, 70s, and 80s. Rosellen was recognized with several awards for her incredible work. One such award was 2007 "Top Dog" as a successful graduate of California State University, Fresno. Another was "Woman of The Year," awarded by the California State Legislature.

Many of the local politicians from the City Council and the County Board of Supervisors, as well as state officials, went to her for advice and support.

If any organization had questions on interpreting the "Roberts Rules of Order" in conducting their meetings, Rosellen Kershaw was the ultimate authority. She settled many a dispute by providing her honest and valued opinion.

Rosellen mentored me as a young man starting a career in local government. She was the one who jump-started my involvement in community service by nominating me to serve on the board of the Fresno County Mental Health Association. When I was in my late thirties, she advised me not to run for Mayor of the City Of Fresno. I never entered the race, which turned out to be the right move.

When my son Bryan and his girlfriend Julie decided to get married, it was a happy time for all of us. Adding family ties to our already existing friendship was a huge plus. Now, a highlight for both of us is sharing two lovely and bright granddaughters, Taylor and Morgan Marsoobian. Fortunately, both inherited their grandmother's and mother's desire and love for reading.

When writing this, Rosellen Kershaw was maybe a few days or a heartbeat away from her last breath, and yes, she was ready. She's ready spiritually, having made a confession of faith and placing her belief in Jesus. She has left her family and several charitable organizations financially strong. She has friends from all over the country, all of whom have only the kindest words to say about her. She is at peace in her relationships with family and friends, and she has lived a life with no regrets.

At the writing of this dedication, Rosellen Kershaw was still hanging on to life. She left us on August 20, 2015. It was my privilege to be with my son and her daughter the night before she took her final breath, as we prayed with and for her. Even though she could not speak in those last days and hours, we could sense her love and the peace she had in leaving. We could see it all in the twinkling of her eye. She will be dearly missed by all the people whose lives she touched.

TABLE OF CONTENTS

PREFACE

"You never truly start to live until you are no longer afraid to die."
                    —**Adrian Rogers**, author and pastor of the
                    "Love Worth Finding" Ministry

We've all heard the phrases:

"Life is short."
"Life is fragile."
"Do it now."
"Make it the best of your time."
"We only have 24 hours a day."
"We all have the same amount of time."
"Don't put off for tomorrow what you can do today."
"We are all a heartbeat away from meeting our Maker."
"Work like you will live forever. Live like you will die today."

I'm sure you can add to this list.

This book is written so that you, the reader, will take a little time to reflect on your life and make sure you are ready for that day when your heart beats for the last time on this earth.

It can happen at any time, any place, and in any number of different ways. A friend of mine, John Savage, a life insurance professional, had two things to say about death when sharing his presentations on the need for life insurance.

"When the black cars with the flags in the front go by, they are not practicing. There's no dress rehearsal."

"When you're dead, you're dead a long time, and you're not coming back."

Both sayings got nervous laughs because we all knew he was correct, but we didn't want to face the facts.

In James 4:13-15, the New International Version of the Bible tells us:

Now listen you who say, "Today or tomorrow we will go to this or that city, spend a year there carry-on business and make money." Why you don't even know what will happen tomorrow. What is your life? You are a mist that appears for a little while and then vanishes. Instead, you ought to say, "If it's the Lord's will, we will live and do this or that."

It is good to have goals, but goals will disappoint us if we leave God out of them. There is no point in making plans as though God does not exist because the future is in His hands. If you put God in the center of your plans, He will never disappoint you.

In Ecclesiastes Chapter 3, Solomon says "There's a time for everything, and a season for every activity under heaven: A time to be born and a time to die."

This is true regardless of your financial status, your religious beliefs, your moral compass, your personality traits, and your ethnic background. We all have the same fate of dying.

The probability of dying is 100%.

How you choose to live your life during the brief time we are here on Earth is a choice God calls "free will." In the movie "Bruce Almighty," the biggest problem that Bruce had when he became God was he couldn't control people's free will and make them love and accept him. He tells GOD that was HIS biggest mistake.

But in reality, it's the one trait humans have over other animal species. Because true love comes when you make it a choice. God wants us to live with Him, but only if we choose to accept His love.

This book is written in three main sections, and each explores what I believe are the three important events that happen each and every time death occurs. The fourth section presents ideas of what you can do while you're still alive to help you and those you love make the transition as painless as possible. These are the sections:

1. Are You Ready Spiritually? (Did you make the right choice for Eternity?)
2. Are You Ready Relationally? (Did you leave with no regrets?)

3. Are You Ready Financially? (Did you leave the right legacy?)

The reality is we have to make these choices before we die. Since we are all "A Heartbeat Away," the sooner we make the right choices the better everyone will be.

In the introduction, you will discover how and why I wrote this book.

INTRODUCTION

(Why I felt compelled to write this book)

"The graveyards are full of great men and women who never became great because they did not give their ability responsibility."
—**Myles Monroe**

It was December 21, 1999, and there was much talk about the millennium coming. People all over the world were concerned about what was going to happen to the computers, to the world of communication, when the clock struck twelve and we moved from the 20th to the 21st century. For me, I was concerned with what was going to happen the next day.

It was December 22, 1999, my 65th birthday, and I was facing major open-heart surgery. The reason this was no ordinary bypass surgery was that it was the second such surgery within seventy days. The head of cardiac surgery at UCLA Medical Center concluded that surgery could be performed, but at a very high risk. The night before the surgery, lying in the warm hospital bed that had been my home for the past week, my thoughts turned to prayer and God. Wanting to have somebody near me who had better connections to the receiver of prayers, I reached out to a young pastor friend, David T. Moore. He was around thirty-six years of age and was head pastor for a large church in Palm Desert, California. We were close enough that I could call him on his cell phone and ask for his prayers.

What he said before the prayer stuck with me and inspired the title of this book. "Arsen, I will be happy to pray for you, but the truth is I am just as close to death as you are."

"What did you say?" I asked surprised.

"We are all just a heartbeat away from meeting Jesus. You're just more aware of it because of what you're facing tomorrow."

"A Heartbeat Away" sounded a little funny at first, causing me to laugh nervously. However, after reality set in, that simple phrase struck me as being very profound. People in a coma, people who had a stroke, people in ICU on life support, people in cancer wards and treatment centers, people in hospice care are all coming to grips with the fact that their lives on this earth are coming to an end. And they and their loved ones are making the appropriate plans. There are the final arrangements to be made; there are financial considerations; there are people you want to say goodbye to; and you may have to make matters right with business partners, friends, or family members. The list could be endless.

There is always a spiritual issue when facing death. Regardless of religious beliefs, everyone wants to truly know what's next.

The priest comes in to give the last rites, pastors come and asked if you've asked for forgiveness, and they want to know if you have Jesus in your heart. Other religions have similar ways and questions for the followers of their belief. Some have no belief in the afterlife, and are just prepared to stop breathing and accept whatever happens.

The point is that some people are lucky to have time to make final plans and to say goodbye. Far too many lives are over in an instant—an accident, an act of violence, choking on a piece of meat, stopping breathing for no apparent reason, or the most common, a heart attack. Yes, the truth is you are only a heartbeat away from leaving this earth.

This story of one man's sudden death also influenced me to write this book. He was an acquaintance, whom I was considering doing business with. Our paths had just crossed a few months earlier. His name was John Merrill Riding. He was a healthy person, about fifty years old and a former volleyball coach who exercised regularly. He also spent time leading Bible studies and activities at Christian youth groups. John and his family were out on a Sunday to play a little family volleyball. His two daughters were volleyball players in college so this was usual for them.

It was a nice summer day and not especially hot, as it can get in Fresno. John stopped to get a drink of water in between matches when he felt a little dizzy and collapsed by the water fountain. His daughters quickly called 911. The ambulances and paramedics were there quickly to do what they were trained to do, but it was too late. My new friend had left this earth quickly and silently, in a blink of an eye. Without as much as a goodbye, his life on earth was over, and his families' lives were changed forever.

His memorial service was attended by nearly twelve hundred people. This is what his wife wrote about John in the memorial announcement: "John lived intentionally. He always looked upward and lived life outward. The man you knew would have been nothing without Christ, and that is what he wanted you to know about him."

As I sat in that memorial service and reflected on how quickly his life had ended, I remembered what my pastor had told me the night before my surgery in 1999, that "we are all a heartbeat away from meeting the Lord." This man's passing made me realize the truth in the pastor's words given to me fifteen years earlier. It became real to me at that moment.

When I left that memorial service, I knew this book had to be written, and I knew what the title would be. What I didn't know was what I had to say beyond the title and this story.

ARE YOU READY SPIRITUALLY?

Spirituality means different things to different people. It brings different images to mind, everything from monks in a monastery, to India yoga masters, priests, Saints, new age mystics … you can finish the list. The purpose of this section is to help the reader consider his or her spirituality as it relates to answering the question most adults ask, "What life is all about and what happens when this brief time on earth is over? My perspective on how to answer this question comes from my reading and understanding of the Holy Bible. It includes both the old and the new testaments. I view the Bible as the infallible Word of God, fully inspired and without error in the original manuscripts, written under the inspiration of the Holy Spirit.

It is not an endorsement of a particular form of religion or denominations within Christianity. It is about having a personal relationship with God through His son Jesus Christ. I believe Jesus died for us so we can have a living, personal relationship with God. This section is meant to give you facts and information so you can make up your own mind on this vital question: Who is Jesus?

In Genesis 1: 26-27 it says, Then God said, "Let us make man in our image, in our likeness, and let them rule over the fish of the sea and the birds of the air, over the livestock, over all the earth, and over all the creatures that move along the ground." So God created man in his own image in the image of God he created him; male and female he created them. Then in Genesis 2:7 the Word continues, The Lord God formed the man from the dust of the ground and breathed into his nostrils the breath of life, and the man became a living being."

The image of GOD is not that we look like Him, but that we have a mind like God that allows us to reason, to create, to love, and experience all the other characteristics of God. Our very breath comes from God. In the end, our breath is the last thing that leaves our body before it returns to a lifeless shell.

Dr. Deepak Chopra, in his book "How to Know GOD: The Soul's Journey Into the Mystery of Mysteries." Harmony Books, 2000, he says. "In the reality sandwich of physics there are also three levels: Material reality, the world of objects and events; Quantum reality, a transition zone where energy turns into matter; Virtual reality, the place beyond time and space, the origin of the universe." He then changes the word "reality" to "domain" for both Quantum and Virtual because of the current use and meanings of those terms. He goes on to say, "If we only knew it, God's most cherished secrets are hidden inside the human skull—ecstasy, eternal love, grace, and mystery. "There is no misconception on my part that I am a Dr. Chopra, or a religious monk, or a yoga Gaur or a rabbi.

The chapters that follow cover my stories, studies, experiences, and beliefs.

Chapter 1

BLINK OF AN EYE

(Stories of real people whose lives ended quickly)

"Live life fully every day, love with all your heart, and always be prepared—we don't know when our time here is finished."
—**Lynn L. Lambrecht**, author

As a young boy of fifteen, I experienced the impact of death for the first time when my father died in a blink of an eye. My mom and dad had separated, and he was not living at home. It was a cold, overcast early morning, October 31, 1950, in Fresno, California. Kids were preparing for Halloween activities. My dad, age 55, finished his breakfast and was on his way to his barbershop, which he was so proud of.

It was only six months since he had opened his own shop. It had taken him more than four years and thousands of dollars to get a California barber's license. He had been cutting hair since coming to America as a teenager, but could not pass the written examination required by the State of California. He had never learned how to read and write English.

Dad had a previous brush with death in 1945, just after World War II ended. During the war years, he worked as a barber at the Fort Ord Army Base in Monterey, California. This was until he had his own small shop on an Army base in Fresno, California, called Hammer Field.

There were no stents, bypass surgery, or other modern heart medicine at that time. Diet, exercise, and reducing stress were the remedies of the day. My dad didn't do any of them. Then, only five years later, while backing the car out of the driveway, he suffered a massive coronary thrombosis, resulting in his immediate death. The car kept moving in reverse, across the street and into the hedge of the neighbor's yard. A young boy on his way to school noticed the car in the bushes with the motor running and a man slumped over the steering wheel. Scared, the boy ran into a stranger's house yelling for someone to help. By the time the ambulance and the police arrived, my father was dead. No time to say goodbye. No time to leave instructions. No will, no life insurance. Just silence.

There was no Halloween celebration in our home that year. To this very day, Halloween is an annual reminder of how fragile life is. Even though there are more effective modern medicines and procedures to repair the heart today than there were in 1950, people die with doctors and paramedics right next to them.

Just like my friend, Ron Wagley.

We met when he was my boss at a major life insurance company. He was one of the vice presidents in charge of field agent development. We worked together through his promotion to Senior Vice President. He eventually was promoted to President of the company where he held that position for five years before he retired to a quiet life.

He was a Christian, and practiced and promoted his faith by holding Bible studies for young businessmen in his home on a regular basis. One Saturday morning, during one of the early morning Bible studies in his home, he started to experience some chest pains. Out of precaution, 911 was called. Once the paramedics arrived and were putting him into the ambulance for a ride to the hospital, his wife of forty-five years asked, "Want me to come with you?" Ron replied, "No, you finish up the Bible study and breakfast. You can come later."

There was no later. My friend, age seventy-two, never made it to the hospital. He died during the journey. The paramedics had everything they needed to save his life, but he was gone to meet his Lord before they could do anything to prevent it. His death occurred five years and six months after his retirement, which by the way, is the average stated length of time between retirement and death according to actuarial studies done by life insurance companies. There will be more about life expectancy in Section III, "Leaving a Legacy."

In another case, there was no call for help, no witness, no illness, no indication that this was her last day on earth. It is a story of a young lady by the name of Jamie. She was only forty-two years of age, and a single mom with a daughter just weeks away from graduating high school. Jamie had a good job in real estate and a nice home with her life in front of her. Jamie was the daughter of a lady I had met as an insurance client, Mrs. E. Ruth

Williams. We are still very close friends even though we live 300 miles apart. This would be Mrs. Williams' second loss of a child.

For Jamie, it was a normal day. Jamie and her daughter shared breakfast while talking about college opportunities, before her daughter went off to school. Jamie prepared to go to work and was making plans to meet her mother later that day to discuss an upcoming birthday party. After work and before her daughter came home from school, Jamie went into her bedroom to change clothes and get ready to meet her mother.

When the daughter arrived home, she found her mother on the bed, motionless and starting to turn cold to the touch. Jamie had passed on to another world within a short period of time, quietly and peacefully with no drama, no sign of violence or drugs. The coroner stated the cause of death was "natural causes." Translation for a forty-two year old person: her heart stopped pumping blood to the rest of her body. This was not called a heart attack. No damage was done to the heart. There was no blood found in any of her cavities. One moment she was fine and full of life, the next she was in another life. This is a very rare form of death and comes very quickly. Her mother said, "God wanted Jamie to come home for some reason." Fortunately, she had a great relationship with her daughter, her mother, and the other family members.

The only good news was that years before she had purchased a $500,000 life insurance policy, which allowed her daughter to go on to college and start her life.

There were many confused and sad people at the funeral. "It happened so fast and unexpectedly" were the comments heard most often. We all expect death to be a lengthy process and come at an older age. I thought my dad was old at fifty-five when I was fifteen. I thought Jamie was young at forty-two when I was seventy-five.

While I was thinking this was a very strange circumstance, my daughter called to tell me the tragic story of a twenty-one year old girlfriend of hers who went to sleep and simply never woke up. She was fine when she went to bed. Autopsy revealed no known cause of death. The death certificate reads "natural causes."

Every day in every major city in America, we read in the newspaper about someone's life ending with a gunshot, in an auto or plane accident, or even from an accident at home. Thousands get up every morning starting their lives with the full expectation that they'll be able to go to bed that night in their own bed. And hundreds of thousands, if not millions, wake up the next morning to start the process over again. But there are thousands more that we never hear about, who never get up for the next day. Were they and their families ready? Contrast this with the lucky person who has time to get his or her affairs in order, say goodbye to family and friends, and get ready for the next journey of life.

One such friend was a lady called Lou. We met later in life when I joined a bowling team in 2010. In retirement, bowling was her and her husband's recreation and a major part of their lives. Lou continued to bowl even after Bob became confined to a wheelchair and she was taking care of him.

Lou was raised in a Christian home, maintained her faith, and believed in Jesus as her savior right up until the end. The end is where this story starts. After several years of battling with cancer, Lou was losing the fight on a daily basis. She was now in hospice care in a makeshift hospital room in her son's living room. The family and friends had gathered around. A sister had traveled from across the country to be with her. I called the house to see how Lou was and if I could come by and visit. Her daughter said I could come by, but she had been asleep for most of the last two days and was not speaking. In reality, the visit was more for me than her, so I went by to pay my respects to the family and my friend. When I arrived, she was as the daughter said, in a deep sleep, motionless even as people were talking, laughing and telling stories about memorable times with their mom, sister, and friend.

As I took her hand in mine, saying a silent prayer, she turned her head slowly toward me with her eyes opened slightly and a smile on her lips.

"Understand you have been sleeping a lot," I said softly in her ear. She just nodded yes. "Have you been dreaming?" I asked. A quiet "yes" came from her tired body. The next question just popped out of my mouth. "Are they good dreams?" I said with a little laughter in my voice.

With the loudest, strongest voice anyone had heard in days came her answer, stopping all conversation in the room. "OH YEAH!"

"I love you, Lou."

"Love you, too," she said in a whisper. She closed her eyes to retreat to those beautiful peaceful dreams. Her daughter called in the morning with the word that she had left to be with her Lord. She thanked me for coming by, saying "Our mother never spoke another word after your conversation. OH YEAH was the last thing we heard her say." How cool is that for last words?

What a testimony she gave at the very end. She had a glimpse of where she was going, and she was so excited to share it with us. I will never forget that experience, and I asked her family for permission to share it here in my book. I also had the privilege of sharing it at her memorial service a few weeks later.

In the preface of the book, I make the statement that life is short and can end at any moment or it can take years. All of these stories are told to make the point that life might end quickly or you might have time to say goodbye. They involved real people who I knew and loved. Without a true belief that you are only "A Heartbeat Away," the rest of the book on how and why you need to get ready will fall short of its intended purpose: moving you to take action and be ready.

Chapter 2

ONE MAN'S JOURNEY

(This is my testimony about
my relationship with Jesus.)

"If life is an accident, it cannot conceivably have any purpose, for accident and purpose are mutually exclusive."
—**John Blanchard**, bestselling author

M y journey and relationship with Jesus started when I was fifteen years old. It was at a Christian summer camp between my sophomore and junior years in high school. No big deal right; this is the age at which the majority of people hear about Jesus and make a decision. It was a big deal for me because I wasn't a member of the denomination hosting the camp.

Let's back up a few years. Growing up, my church experience as a young boy was attending Sunday school at the Holy Trinity Armenian Apostolic Church. My mom and I went on special occasions, but I never saw my dad grace the grounds, let alone enter the doors of the church. The closest thing he came to a reference of a spiritual nature was when he would take his hat off as he drove by any church. When I asked him why he did this, he told me he was showing respect for God and His house.

A year after my father's passing, a neighbor buddy of mine invited me to go to a Sunday youth group meeting at the First Methodist Church. Not being sure of my mother's reaction to going to non-Armenian Church, I approached her, bringing along my friend for backup. We were both pleased when she said, "As long as you are going to hear about God, you can go." This was a welcome and unexpected response.

My motives were not the same as my mother's. My friend had explained the program to me earlier. We play basketball for an hour and a half, the ladies cook us a nice meal, and then we hang out with the girls afterward. To a teenage boy, this was a great idea of a church. If the price I had to pay for all the fun stuff was to listen to stories about some olden times and people, it was worth it.

The next logical step in hanging out with my buddies was going to a Christian summer camp. I thought this was going to simply be an extension of Sunday evenings. In many ways it was: fun, games, good food, and once it was over, hanging out with the girls.

What I didn't count on was meeting a special young girl from a town 110 miles from Fresno. We met in a strange way. A friend needed some medical attention so I went with him to the infirmary. As soon as we walked in, she attracted my attention. The room was full and the nurses were overloaded, so I was more than willing to help the nurse attend to her patients. She was a year older than I was, and she really didn't want much to do with a skinny kid from Fresno. However, I made it my mission to be in every event she was in. I did everything I could to be close to her. Then one day she asked if I wanted to join her on the voluntary hike up to the mountaintop at sunset. It was high enough where we could almost see the Pacific Ocean between all of the beautiful redwood trees. That chilly evening, the stories of old-timers included the message of Jesus and of the need to be born again. When the invitation was given to ask God for the forgiveness of my sins and to come into my life, I bowed my head with one eye on the special girl. She had her head bowed, both eyes closed, and was praying. So I did the same thing. No big fireworks and no tingling sensation, but I had invited Jesus into my heart. I didn't know it at that time, but my life would be changed forever.

The summer ended, but my interest in this "special girl" didn't. We tried a long distance romance, but it never developed into anything more than a lifelong friendship. When I get to heaven, I am going to look her up. My friend went to be with the Lord after losing her battle with cancer over 30 years ago.

After that summer, my life started to improve on many levels. In athletics, I started winning races and breaking both school records and Central Valley records. In the mile races, I would pray, "God, you pick 'em up, and I will lay them down," referring to my legs. Well, he answered my prayers so many times that this poor Armenian kid with no idea what to do with his life was given a scholarship to Fresno State College. Through HIS continued support, I received a degree in physical education, a California secondary teaching credential, and four

Varsity letters as a two miler on the track team. As a four-year Varsity letterman, I never won a race, but I did add points to the team meets. The reward for my participation was a life pass allowing me free access to all Fresno State University athletic events, an education, and a pathway to life.

In the spiritual world, things improved there as well. I started to enjoy and understand the messages in a clear way. When I prayed at night, I thought I could actually see a figure in the distance that looked like Jesus in a robe. My prayers were conversations. Jesus was real, and He didn't care that I may have had a different reason for praying that summer night. He knew I needed Him more than I did. He showed His love for me by saving me even though I was still a sinner.

I wish I could say my relationship and spiritual journey continued to grow without a break. However, that's not what happened. After college, my first full-time job was out of Fresno, as a recreation therapist at Camarillo State Mental Hospital in Southern California. I stopped going to church or having any contact with Christians, and started to grow as an adult.

During the next several years, everything seemed to go along normally and each new job brought something better. I even fell in love with a beautiful redheaded Armenian girl from Fresno. We dated for eleven months before we got married, and we had three beautiful children within 18 months of each other, Brad, Lori and Bryan. I started a 20-year career with the City of Fresno Government, and I was involved in civic and social activities. As a married couple, we started to attend the church we were married in, Holy Trinity Armenian Apostolic Church. We both grew up in this church. Going to church consisted of holidays and special occasions, maybe three or four times a year. It was more for social and religious activities than it was a spiritual experience.

By 1972, I was the perfect picture of secular success, a Deputy City Manager of the City of Fresno, on special assignment to the Mayor, selected the "Outstanding Young Man of Fresno." I was in leadership positions and serving in several community organizations. I made thousands of acquaintances, but no true friends. I had all the material possessions one man could want: a large home with a swimming pool, a Cadillac, and including man's best friend a dog renamed Rusty. I thought I was a good guy, good husband, and good father. So why was I so unhappy and wondering what life was all about? I would ask myself, "Am I doing the right thing with my life?"

Then an incident occurred on the evening of Mother's Day, 1972, that caused me to re-examine my relationship with God. Here is what happened that evening. I had brought my mother-in-law home from a nice Mother's Day event at my sister-in-law's house. My family was in the car. We had parked in front of my mother-in-law's house, which was on a busy Fresno street.

I had gotten out of the car and was bent over into the trunk, retrieving my mother-in-law's belongings, when a women who was drunk, slammed into the backside of my car at a speed of 50-60 miles an hour, just grazing my pants leg. A witness to the accident, riding in car a few yards behind the speeding car, told the police and me that she saw the woman's car come out of the parking lot of a bar and drive along the curb at a high rate of speed, headed straight for me. She said the car drove like this for at least two blocks. She said she knew I didn't see the car coming when I got out of my car, so she closed her eyes, said a prayer, and made the sign of the cross. After hearing the sound of the impact, which blew out the left rear tire and sent my hubcap flying forward 200 feet down the street, she said she opened her eyes and couldn't believe I was still standing there in one piece. We all agreed it was through the grace of God that not only did the car miss me but no one was seriously hurt in my car, and the driver of the car that hit us wasn't seriously hurt. After this incident, God had my attention. It also proved to be a major turning point in our lives.

I started to return to the Armenian Church on a regular basis. I was praying, lighting candles, offering my services to help at the church functions. I became youth director for the junior and senior high school groups at the church. In a few years, I was Chairman to the Board of Trustees. I was serving the church, but I was a long way from a spiritual relationship with God. My lifestyle really hadn't changed. I was still working hard at my job, and being a dad and husband. Yet there was emptiness in my life.

This lasted about five years. I still didn't know what God wanted me to do with my life. My marriage started to have problems that resulted in me making several bad choices. The main one was falling in love and having an affair with a lady from the Armenian Church. In the course of three years, I experienced a bitter divorce, resigned the Chairmanship of the Church Board of Trustees, and stranded my relationship with my children. At this time, I also left my position at the City of Fresno to take on responsibilities as the executive director of the fundraising division of Fresno State University Athletics. What

I thought would be a lifelong commitment lasted only thirteen months before my contract was up and not renewed.

At the age of forty-five, I was facing personal and professional rejection for the first time. In those years of poor choices, I went from being on top of the world to a life that was out of control. I was unemployed, unmarried, and uninterested in everything; however, I still maintained a level of dignity and self-confidence. One major blessing was that my oldest son, Brad, came to live with me. Being a single parent kept me grounded and close to my children. I started a new career in life insurance that I am still doing. After six years of dating, I married the lady I left my wife for. We drove over to Las Vegas with a couple of friends for the weekend. The marriage lasted only five and half months and ended in an annulment. During this time, there was no church or spiritual connection in my life at all.

Within nine months of the annulment, my friend and second wife was diagnosed with lung cancer. The battle lasted just six months, and during that time, we would spend time together almost every day. It was a time of reflection, and I would read the Bible to her, looking for answers to the question of what happens next. However, I didn't know what to read or how to explain what I had read. I know now that one first needs to have faith before you get the help of the Holy Spirit to guide your thoughts as you read the Bible. When she died at age fifty-two, I felt like a failure—empty, helpless and very sad not knowing for sure where she was spending eternity.

My life insurance business at this point was up and down, but mostly down. I had switched companies and met a man and a woman who would become very special to me. God was working in my life, but I didn't realize it at the time. All my focus was on me, and I could not see Him.

Through a series of events, which would be a book in itself, I was invited to a luncheon by a life insurance broker of mine named Ed Hamill. The lunch was being hosted by an organization called the Christian Business Man Committee, or CBMC. It is now called Christian Business Man Connection. This was November of 1985, eleven months after my friend's passing. The speaker at the event was the national director of the organization, Ted DeMoss. At the end of his presentation, he invited anyone who wanted to know about Jesus and gain salvation to say a prayer that he offered. He also reminded anyone, like me, who had prayed before but needed to be recommitted to pray the same prayer. That is exactly what I did.

After this luncheon, I started attending CBMC weekly lunches and got to know the men associated with the local committee. Another life insurance agent by the name of Tom Sommers asked if I wanted to go through a one-on-one Bible study with him called "Operation Timothy." At the age of fifty-one, I started to read God's Word for the first time in a systematic way—to understand who God is, who the man Jesus is, to decide if the Bible is reliable, and learn what it means to be a Christian. The books and guidelines are designed for a 16-week study. However, because of questions and personal issues, it took us three years, meeting once a week, before we finished the program.

What has life been like for the last thirty years since I reconnected my life to Christ? For the first four years, my spiritual life was growing through CBMC activities and participation in the Evangelical Free Church of Fresno with my youngest son Bryan and his girlfriend, and now wife, Julie Kershaw. My mother started attending with me, along with my daughter Lori. One special Sunday evening, I witnessed my mother at age eighty-seven make a confession of faith and accept Jesus into her life. When she passed away a year later, my feelings at her funeral were love, fulfillment, and the satisfaction of knowing she is waiting in Paradise for me and her family.

My first wife and I , after that bitter divorce ten years earlier, were reconciled to the point that we were able to date for a few years, and we even considered being remarried after she accepted Jesus as her personal savior. It didn't work out, but we are still friends and look out for one another even until today. We currently each have our own lives with our major interest centered on the grandchildren.

In July of 1989, my life would take another major turn. This one took me away from my Christian friends and the community I had lived and worked in for fifty-five years. It all started when through a series of events, another woman came into my life unexpectedly. It was during an Armenian Fourth of July dance festival, in Boston, Massachusetts, that lasted for three days. Within four months of meeting and keeping in contact mostly by phone, I was so much in love with this woman that I accepted a job as Sales and Marketing Director for the large life insurance company for which I was a general agent in Fresno. This job required me to sell my business, move to the East Coast, and take over the direction of Transamerica Life Insurance Agencies in the New England states.

One month after starting my new life, the woman of my dreams said it was over between us. In the next thirteen years, I would have fifteen addresses, get married to a Catholic woman from Massachusetts with two children in high school and one graduating from college. I loved those children as though they were mine. This marriage also changed my life direction and lasted seven and half years. Before we got married she made a confession of faith, but we never found a church home during our time together. The closest we came was attending a charismatic church while living in Nashville, Tennessee, for three years. We divorced in February 2001, and I moved back to Fresno. She moved back to Massachusetts where she remarried eighteen months later.

Of all the blessings I have had in the last thirty years, the one I consider the most important is my association with Christians from several different denominations. I have met and worshiped with God's people from Eastern Orthodox churches, Protestant churches, Evangelical churches, Charismatic churches, and non-denominational community-based Bible Teaching churches. Each has its own set of traditions, guidelines, and rules. All have the foundation of the resurrection of Jesus and the belief in the Trinity of God the Father, God the Son, and God the Holy Spirit. However, each has one of the three more prominent in its following and a different method of Baptism. For me, I have been baptized in all three methods. I was sprinkled as a baby in the Armenian Apostolic Church. I was baptized in water submersion at the Evangelical Free Church of Fresno in October 1989, and I was baptized in the Holy Spirit at a Charismatic Church in Nashville, Tennessee.

Since returning to Fresno in 2001, I have become active in the Fresno chapter of CBMC where I continue to learn by reading, studying, and praying for guidance in my life for as long as God keeps me on this earth. Tom Sommers retired from the business of life insurance, and he is now the full-time Executive Director of Fresno CBMC and CBWC.

To summarize, my life and walk with God is not much different from anyone else's. We are born into a family that may or may not believe in God or Jesus. We grow up learning and doing what others around us are doing, until our lives are impacted by someone or something that shifts our thinking. You start to grow into life, education, jobs, relationships, marriage, family, good times, bad times, sickness, deaths of family and friends.

The question of what life is all about will arise for everyone at some point, which becomes a transformational point in time. I made a choice to put my faith and belief into Jesus. Once this decision was made, there was a continual transformational shift in my thinking, my awareness in behavior patterns, and my relationships. I spent a lot of time drifting in and out of relationship with God, but He never moved. The spiritual part of life is very personal. It is not a family, community, ethnic, or cultural decision.

If you are reading this and have never asked Jesus into your life, take a time out and settle your salvation. Decide how you are going to live your life on earth for as long as you are here.

Pray something like this: *Jesus, I acknowledge that you are the Son of God, that you died for my sins, rose from the grave on the third day, and are seated at the right hand of God. I ask YOU to forgive me of my sins, the past, present and the future and to come into my heart and be the Lord of my life. Amen.*

Chapter 3

IN OR OUT

(How many ways are there to get into heaven?)

"I am the way, the truth and the life. No one comes to the Father except through me."
—**John 14:6**, the Bible NIV

Some of you may still have questions about why this is the only way to get into heaven and have eternal life with God. I understand this completely. My brother, who is fourteen years older than I am, questioned me regarding this point for most of our adult lives. I loved my brother, and I did all I could to explain it to him. I showed him in the Bible why I was telling him the truth. Thirty minutes before he took his last breath in an emergency hospital room, his son Brent asked him if he believed in Jesus as his Lord and Savior, and all he had done for him, he said he did. When I arrived at the hospital, my brother was gone from this world, but I know we will see each other again.

It was the same for my sister. It wasn't until she was facing death that she made a decision to accept the truth and free gift of salvation through God's grace. They missed a lifetime of joy in knowing Jesus but are with Him now. Don't wait. You are just a heartbeat away from losing out on the greatest gift of your life.

At one point in the conversation with my brother, who was a gambler, I asked him about the risk of the gamble he was taking by rejecting this truth. He said, "If I am right and there is no need for salvation and everyone goes to heaven, then I've had a lot of fun in my life doing what I want. I have been a good person. I win. But if you're right and I'm wrong and the Bible is true and Jesus is the only way, then that would be a big loss."

If you think this is still too narrow a way of thinking and that a loving God, the creator of all things, must have provided other ways into heaven, listen to what Jesus said when asked this question: "I am the way, the truth and the life. No one comes to the Father except through me. If you had really known me, you would know who my father is. From now on, you do know Him and have seen Him!" (New International Version [NIV] of the Bible. John 14: 6-7)

Here is a question to ponder. How many ways did God give us to get into this world? The woman carries the egg which needs to be united with but one sperm; it is estimated there are 50,000 sperm fighting to be the winner, to create life and then to bring it into this world. She alone is the passage into this world, and that passage is very narrow and very specific. So why is it so difficult to believe that it's just as narrow and difficult to return to God as it was coming into this world. It makes logical sense to me. He made one way into this life, through the body of the mother. Why then question when He says there is only one way back to Him, through His son's body.

God loves everyone. He created and wants everyone to use his or her own free will and accept His gift of salvation. John 3:16 shows us just how much God loves us all. He sent His Son as a sacrifice to atone for our sins. We just need to believe and accept this truth.

My long-time friend and Fresno State legendary baseball coach, Pete Beiden, said from his hospital bed when finally accepting this truth, "We get so much, and we have to do so little." You won once to get here. Why not be a winner again before you leave? Make sure your passport has the right credentials to get you in.

In a few chapters, we are going to take a closer look at where and what we can expect when we get to heaven. After all, if you were going to take a trip to a foreign country, wouldn't you want to get a travel guide and read about the place you're going? Wouldn't you want to know the route you were going to take and any necessary stops before you got to your final destination?

However, before getting into the next chapters where I explain the basis for my faith in Jesus and the difference between religion and a spiritual relationship with God, I want to give you time to consider your current position with God and the sample prayer we ended the last chapter with.

"Jesus, I acknowledge that you are the Son of God, that you died for my sins, rose from the grave on the third day, and are seated at the right hand of God. I ask YOU to forgive me of my sins, the past, present and the future and to come into my heart and be the Lord of my life. Amen."

Chapter 4

FROM HERE TO ETERNITY

(A short version and understanding of Heaven)

"So we fix our eyes not on what is seen, but on what is unseen.
For what is seen is temporary, but what is unseen is eternal."
—2nd Corinthians 4:18, The Bible, NIV

W hen I talk about the fact that you're only a heartbeat away from meeting the Lord, some people make the statement that they're not going to meet the Lord because they're not religious. It's not about being religious. It's about having a spiritual relationship with the God of the Universe and His son, Jesus Christ.

If we claim to be without sin, we deceive ourselves and the truth is not in us. If we confess our sins, He is faithful and just and will forgive us our sins and purify us from all unrighteousness. (1 John 1:8-9) Those who have put their faith in Jesus Christ have been made righteous in the eyes of God, all their past, present and future sins have been forgiven and forgotten.

God is HOLY and therefore cannot be in the presence of sin. Everyone born of a man and woman is born with sin. Therefore, to live in God's presence for eternity, you must have your sins forgiven before you leave this world.

Then HOW TO DO THIS? This is the biggest question that has divided people with different religious beliefs for thousands of years.

God first chose a righteous man called Abram, changed his name to Abraham, and at the age of one hundred gave him a son, Isaac. God then told Abraham to kill Isaac as a blood offering to show his faithfulness to God. The importance of the shedding of blood to become right with God was established. However, before he could carry out the act, God intervened and gave him a ram to sacrifice instead. God then promised him more descendants than there are stars in the sky. These people would come through Isaac. Jesus was born from these Jewish people.

As God's only son, He was offered as a blood offering to make it possible for all mankind to be made righteous and able to be in God's presence. The first step is having faith in Jesus and what happened to Him.

If it's important to place one's faith in Jesus, to have eternal life, then there is a need to know what "faith" is. Many people want to have all the facts before making any decision, let alone one that will determine where their spirits will spend eternity. The question then becomes if you can have faith and facts at the same time. To me, if I get all the facts first, then I don't need faith. When it comes to spiritual issues, and the use of the Bible as the reference, this complicates the discussion even more. From my experience, after I placed my faith in the miracle of the resurrection of Jesus, then the facts in the Bible that prove this event made sense to me. You have faith first then verify what you believe with facts.

There are probably hundreds of thousands of books written on the subject of Jesus's death and resurrection. Two that I would recommend reading are by author Lee Strobel, *The Case for Christ*, and *The Case for Faith*. Another book I used for research, by the same author is *The Case for Christianity Answer Book*, which was published in 2014. All of these books and more can be found on his website, www.Leestrobel.com.

Based on historical records, there is no question but that a Jewish man named Jesus was born and lived in the Middle East. History also recorded that He performed many miracles and spoke with intelligence and authority about the Jewish laws. His teachings attracted thousands to him, but He selected twelve men who were called His disciples and several women followers who He cared for their needs as well.

This man called Jesus caused a great uprising and was very troubling to the Jewish governing body called the Sanhedrin. The big issue was whether Jesus had claimed to be the "Son of Man," and God's Son, which made him equal to God. These claims were considered blasphemy, and under Jewish law were punishable by death. The only problem was the Jews lived under the rule of the Roman Empire, and only the Roman Governor could sentence anyone to death. For details and information on the politics of the Roman Empire during that time, and historical facts surrounding this event, you may want to read *Killing Jesus*, by Bill O'Reilly and Martin Dugard, and published by Henry Holt and Company, of New York.

Most likely, you have lived long enough to have heard the Easter Story. The one about the crucifixion, burial and resurrection three days later of the man called Jesus. This historical event, which took place approximately 2000 years ago, changed the world and how people viewed themselves and others. Whether or not you believe Jesus was who He said He was, you cannot deny the historical reality of the event on that weekend. It just can't be ignored.

Christianity is based on the one event told in the rest of the story—His resurrection from the dead after being in a sealed tomb for three days. As hard as it is to believe, this was Jesus' reason for being born of a virgin. He was born without the same sin we inherit from the first man God created, Adam. Jesus's birth, life, death, and resurrection were prophesied 800 years before he was born by the Prophet Isaiah.

How do I know this? Yes, it is written in all the versions of the Bible, in both the Old and New Testaments. Without getting into a discussion on the validity of the Bible (which would be another book), allow me to point out a few facts I learned from reading Lee Strobel's books.

Let's start by going back to the twelve Jewish men who were called Disciples. These were ordinary people, not religious leaders, but followers of the Jewish religion. Most made a living as hard working fishermen. There was Simon called Peter and his brother Andrew, two other brothers James and John whose father was Zebedee. These were the first four Jesus asked to join him on His journey. They had heard of Him and what He had been doing, so they left their jobs and daily lives to follow Jesus. Two would become key figures in our story, Peter and John. Then there was Matthew, a tax collector. Tax collectors were known to be tough men and sometimes corrupt. They were part of the outcast group but were known to be wealthy. So for Matthew, following Jesus was both good and bad news. He gave up wealth but gained a new status in the community by joining a new group. As a tax collector, Matthew had to keep reports so he knew how to write effectively. The other men called were Philip, Bartholomew, Thomas, Thaddeus, Simon the Zealot (a political activist), another James, the son of Alphaeus, and Judas Iscariot.

Now Judas, who served as the treasurer of the group, became notorious because he was the one who betrayed Jesus for twenty pieces of silver. Afterwards, he felt so guilty that he committed suicide. The Jewish prophet Isaiah also prophesied this event thousands of years before when predicting the events by which man would know the Messiah. It is important to remember that these twelve people were ordinary with modest means, living their lives one day at a time just like you and me today.

Now back to the story of Jesus' death, burial and resurrection, and how we can know it is true. Because if this is not true, the hundreds of millions of people who have lived and died since Jesus walked on Earth have believed the biggest lie and hoax ever conceived.

We have a leader of a gang of twelve who is arrested for starting a rebellion against the current respected learned leaders of a religious group that has followed the God of the Universe for thousands of years. These leaders were descendants of Abraham, Jacob, and Isaac, and followers of Moses and the Ten Commandments written by God's own hand. However, they had two major groups: the Pharisees and the Sadducees. The Pharisees were admired by the common man, committed to obeying God's commandments, and they believed in the bodily resurrection, eternal life, angels, and demons. The Sadducees, on the other hand, believed strongly in the Mosaic Law and the Levitical purity and were considered more practical minded than the Pharisees. These two groups made up the governing body called the "Sanhedrin," mentioned earlier. Both of these groups believed their position to be correct and tried to enforce their beliefs on the common man. This division still exists today.

So you can see that Jesus's teaching, and the things He was doing, led many people to follow Him. This was very upsetting to both sides, the Pharisees and the Sadducees. Their authority and control over the Jewish people was being severely challenged by this new teaching of "Love God and love your neighbor as yourself," which Jesus said summed up the Ten Commandments.

Once Jesus was arrested, what happened to the remaining gang of eleven? Yep, you guessed it. They went into hiding. Peter hung out to see what was going to happen. However, when he was recognized and they said that he was one of Jesus' followers, Peter denied even knowing Jesus. This happened three times in a matter of few hours, just as Jesus told Peter it would. Only John dared to join the crowd and go to the crucifixion. The others were still afraid they were going to be arrested, or at least kept from going to the Synagogue and participating in the Holy

Holidays. They retreated to a house and boarded it up so they would not be found.

Their lives must have seemed over. Everything they had experienced and learned in just three short years with Jesus was about to end. They thought they would be leaders in a new Kingdom, but now they were hiding and worried about what would happen next.

Reminds me of a sermon I heard entitled, "It's Friday But Sunday's Coming." Their life looked dark. It was Friday, and they didn't know that Sunday was coming with a whole new role for their lives. A new Holy Holiday was about to happen, one that is still celebrated thousands of years later. Easter.

In addition to the twelve men known as Disciples, there were women also mentioned who followed Jesus and attended to the needs of the group. There was Mary Magdalene, Mary and her sister Martha, and several others not referred to by name. Women didn't have much social standing or voice in public affairs at that time. They were to be seen and not heard. However, Mary Magdalene is important to the rest of the story of Jesus' death, burial and resurrection because she was an eyewitness to all three events. She also had a close relationship with the twelve Disciples. History recorded her being present at the cross when He died. She provided the herbs and ointments to preserve the body, and she was the first to arrive at the open tomb. After confirmation from an angel in the tomb that Jesus had risen and was not there, she ran back to tell the men in the closed-up house what she had just witnessed.

Now, who is going to believe a story like that, especially from a woman? Mary Magdalene was heartbroken and probably wanted to believe anything that would make her feel better after the loss of a loved friend. Don't we want to believe that our loved ones are in a better place, that all is okay, or maybe hope that their death was just a dream?

Remember, that after Jesus was placed in the tomb, it was sealed with a large boulder and then guarded by Roman soldiers. The guards were placed there at the request of the religious leaders because they were afraid that these twelve cowards would somehow come, steal the body, and proclaim that he was alive. They believed twelve men, who wouldn't defend or even come to the funeral, were so brave that they were going to attack Roman soldiers and steal Jesus' body. Even if they could overtake the armed guards, they would have to quickly bury it somewhere that no one else would ever find it. They would also have to do this very quickly as the guards' lives were in jeopardy if anyone got past them.

Many today believe this is what happened to Jesus' body. For centuries, archaeologists have looked all over that area but have found no sign of another burial plot, or the bones of anyone, let alone those belonging to a man called Jesus. All they have found is what the young Jewish women said she saw thousand of years ago, an empty tomb with burial cloths folded where a body once laid.

In disbelief, but with hope in their hearts, John and Peter raced out of the house and ran towards the tomb not knowing what to expect. The Bible story says John was a little faster than Peter and arrived at the tomb first. However, he stopped when he saw the stone had been moved and the tomb opened. Peter ran past him into the tomb, which was large enough to stand up in. He wanted to make sure what Mary had said was true. Yup, no body there. Only folded linen.

"Hey John, let's go back and tell the other nine who are hiding that what Mary was saying is true." However, before they could get back with the news of the empty tomb, Jesus appeared to Mary Magdalene at the tomb. She did not recognize Him until He spoke to her. Now that is really breaking news; a dead man talking. Then Jesus started appearing and talking to the other followers. Two men were walking along talking about the message Mary was spreading when Jesus joined them. They didn't recognize him until He told them that the one they are talking about is He. Can you imagine the looks on their faces when they took a closer look and realized it is Him?

Later that night He appeared to the disciples for the first time. They were behind locked doors and windows for fear of the Jewish leaders. He spoke to them, saying "May peace be with you." He ate with them and talked to them with instructions of what to do, just as he had done in the past. They sent word to Thomas that Jesus was with them and that he should come over. Thomas said he didn't believe it and wouldn't believe it until he saw for himself and put his fingers in the nail holes. However, Thomas would humor them and come over. When he arrived, Jesus told him to put his hands in His side where the spear had pierced Him. "Wow! It is you. Now I believe." I am sure you have heard the saying "Doubting Thomas"? Well, now you know its origin. (For the full Biblical account of these events, go to John 20: 1-30, in the NIV.)

Historians recorded that Jesus walked on the earth for forty days after His resurrection. Jesus appeared and taught the

Disciples on three different occasions. He appeared to over 500 people and performed countless miracles. However, there is no record that He showed himself to the religious leaders. They heard it from the ordinary folks. These same religious leaders did not deny that the tomb was empty. They tried to explain it away with stories of how the body was stolen. Can you imagine the talk going around? "This Jesus guy was who He said He was, God in the flesh. Must have been. How else do you explain Him being alive after we watched Him die on the cross?"

My mother once told me that the mourning period of forty days, when the family is to wear black, was because of Jesus' forty days on Earth after His death. Today some people don't wear black after the funeral for more than forty minutes.

What happened next was the real test of the validity of their stories. Jesus changed them from cowards into the evangelists who lived the rest of their lives proclaiming Jesus' resurrection. They became Apostles who were given direction by Jesus to teach the story first to the people in Jerusalem, Judea, and Samaria, and then to the rest of the world.

How could eleven men pull off such an assignment? Jesus gave them the power to do all the same kinds of miracles that He had done by breathing the Holy Spirit into them. (John 20:22) Jesus gave us an example of strong leadership. He gave them the responsibility to tell the world what they had seen and heard, and he gave them the authority to carry out the task.

At one of Peter's sermons, the one who denied knowing Jesus, 3000 people became followers and believers in Jesus as the Messiah. What happened to change these cowards into preachers and teachers of the risen Jesus? The religious leaders were just as upset with their teachings as they had been with Jesus'. Maybe even more so.

The Sanhedrin rounded up these men, telling the story that they met Jesus after His death, blaming them for causing a rebellion against the Jewish faith with the lie that Jesus was alive. They wanted the penalty for their actions to be death. However, one of the members of the council, who may have believed Jesus was the Messiah, made a statement something like this: If we kill them and they are telling the truth, then we will have to answer to God. If it's just a story to make themselves feel good and get other followers, it will not last. People will figure it out, and in time, it will all go away. The verdict came in. "Instruct them to stop telling this story, and give them a flogging they won't forget, but don't kill them."

Well, they took their beating and kept right on ticking as the story goes. All but John, who was exiled to the Greek island of Patmos, but returned to Ephesus at an old age to die of natural causes, died by stoning or, as Peter, on a cross. However, he requested to be hung upside down, as he did not feel worthy to die the same death as Jesus.

Psychiatrists have said that it is virtually impossible to get twelve people to make up a lie and then have none of them confess the truth when faced with death. Yet that is what these twelve, and others, did. There was a man called Matthias who was elected to replace Judas Iscariot after his death. This way they would have twelve, just as Jesus had selected, to teach the Jewish people that Jesus was the Messiah.

Now, a wealthy member of the Sanhedrin was so upset with this teaching that he got permission from the council of the religious leaders to hunt down and kill anybody who professed to follow this new rebellious religion. His name was Saul, and he came from Tarsus. It was recorded that, in fact, he did have people stoned to death who were preaching the good news. The first man Saul had stoned to death was Stephen.

After about four or five years of Saul's persecution of the followers of the new sect, Jesus appeared to him on one of his trips to the town of Damascus where a number of the main leaders were. The light from the presence of Jesus blinded Saul and terrified those that were with him. Saul was the only one who heard Jesus tell him his name would now be Paul, and he was to take the message of eternal life through faith in Jesus to the non-Jews. He received his sight back when he arrived in Damascus, as one of the followers was instructed by Jesus to welcome him and clean him up. Paul was to be considered one of the Disciples, and he would become an Apostle.

This Jewish religious leader named Saul became the Apostle Paul, the author of 13 books of the New Testament. He was not only a Jew but also a Roman citizen, which gave him special privileges and protection that the other Apostles didn't have. Because he was a Roman citizen, God directed his path to Rome where he shared the story of Jesus with Caesar directly.

Let me close this account by quoting a secular historian that Lee Strobel quotes in his book *The Case for Christianity Answer Book*. "Historian Gary Habermas lists 39 ancient sources outside the Bible that provide more than 100 facts about Jesus's life teachings, death, and resurrection." (*The Historical Jesus*; Nashville: Thomas Nelson, 1988)

Chapter 5

KEYS TO THE GATES
(How to know for sure you
are going to get into heaven?)

*"I tell you the truth. No one can see the kingdom of God unless
he is born again."*
—Jesus the Christ

I n the New International Version (NIV) of the Bible, we are
given the clearest answer to this age-old question: "How
can I know for sure I will go to heaven when I die?" Jesus'
answer is recorded in the book of John, chapter 3, starting
with verse 2 and going through verse 21 (added below for
your convenience). This book in the New Testament of the
Bible was written by Jesus's closest disciple, John. It is one
of the recordings of Jesus' life on earth as witnessed by the
men who lived with him on a daily basis for three years. (The
most famous and surely most quoted passage from the Bible,
John 3:16, is part of this conversation.)

41

"A Pharisee named Nicodemus, who was a Biblical scholar, a member of the Sanhedrin which is the highest ranking Jewish governing body, asked Jesus directly the question everyone wants to know. "How do we get into heaven?"

This meeting with Jesus came under the cover of darkness, as Nicodemus didn't want other members of the Sanhedrin to see him talking to Jesus. The New International Version of the Bible (NIV) translates the conversation like this: "Rabbi, we know you are a teacher who has come from God. For no one could perform the miraculous signs you are doing if God were not with him." In reply, Jesus declared, "I tell you the truth. No one can see the kingdom of God unless he is born again."

"How can a man be born when he is old?" Nicodemus asked. "Surely he cannot enter a second time into his mother's womb to be born!" Jesus answered, "I tell you the truth. No one can see the kingdom of God unless he is born of water and the Spirit. Flesh gives birth to flesh, but the Spirit gives birth to the Spirit. You should not be surprised at my saying, 'You must be born again.' The wind blows wherever it pleases. You hear its sound, but you cannot tell where it comes from or where it is going. So it is with everyone born of the Spirit."

How can this be? Nicodemus asked. "You are Israel's teacher," said Jesus, "and do you not understand these things? I tell you the truth, we speak of what we know, and we testified to what we have seen, but still you people do not accept our testimony. I have spoken to you of earthly things and you did not believe; how then will you believe if I speak of heavenly things? No one has ever gone into heaven except the one who came from heaven—The Son of Man. Just as Moses lifted up the snake in the desert, so the Son of Man must be lifted up, that everyone who believes in him may have eternal life.

"For God so loved the world that he gave his one and only Son, that whoever believes in Him shall not perish but have eternal life. (3:16) For God did not send his Son into the world to condemn the world, but to save the world through Him. Whoever believes in Him is not condemned, but whoever does not believe stands condemned already because he has not believed in the name of God's one and only son.

This is the verdict: Light has come into the world, but men loved darkness instead of light because their deeds were evil. Everyone who does evil hates the light, and will not come into the light for fear that his deeds will be exposed. But whoever lives by the truth comes into the light, so that it may be seen plainly that what he has done has been done through God."

When I say a heartbeat away from "meeting the Lord," it is for those who have placed their faith in Jesus Christ. When the body ceases functioning, at that moment, in a twinkling of an eye, their spirit leaves their bodies and is united with Jesus in Paradise.

If you die without having made this decision, your soul is eternally separated from God and waits for the Great White Throne Judgment by God. The Bible says that at the end of time, all will account for their actions here on Earth.

In the next chapter, we are going to take a closer look at where and what we can expect when we get to heaven. After all, if you were going to take a trip to a foreign country wouldn't you want to get a travel guide and read about the place you're going? You would want to know the route you were going to take and any stops necessary before you arrived at your final destination.

Chapter 6

WHERE ARE YOU GOING?
(What will life be like in heaven,
and is there more than one?)

*"Soon you will read in the newspaper that I am dead. Don't
believe it for a moment. I will be more alive than ever before."*
—**D.L Moody**, theologian and evangelist

I n the last chapter, we covered the fact that everyone is
going to leave this earth at some point. Some become
aware of a possible time frame in which it may happen
while many others never know. The last chapter explained the
importance of knowing where the spirit goes after life stops
on this planet. The last point was how you can know for sure
your spirit will spend eternity in the presence of the One who
made you, God.

So, if the plan and objective are to spend eternity with God,
shouldn't we know a little about what that is going to be like?
The term that we use for God's dwelling place is "Heaven."

The place where the spirits go when separated from God is called Hell. Both locations are mentioned several times in the Bible. Jesus actually spoke more about Hell than he did about Heaven. Heaven is mentioned in 47 of the 66 Books of the Bible. The last two chapters, in the book of Revelation, give us the most information.

What will Hell be like? It will be a place of utter misery (Matthew 13:42; 13:50; 22:13; 24:51; 25:30; and Luke 13:28). "It will be a place of conscious punishment for sins with no hope of relief." This is the place where souls of people who have rejected Jesus on this earth and have faced God's judgment will spend eternity. He will say to them, "Depart from me, you who are cursed, into the eternal fire prepared for the devil and his angels" (Matthew 25:41).

However, assuming you would rather be in Heaven than Hell, the balance of this chapter deals with what we know about Heaven. The choice is always yours.

Since there are many different opinions and interpretations of what the Bible says about Heaven, the research on the subject was interesting and challenging. The points of view that made the most sense to me came from the book *Heaven* by Dr. Randy Alcorn, published in 2004 and available on amazon.com.

Dr. Alcorn, as a pastor, started studying the subject over thirty years ago. He eventually founded the nonprofit organization "Eternal Perspective Ministries," or EPM, in 1990. You can look it up online at www.epm.org. He has authored over twenty-five books on this subject. His book *Safely Home* was awarded the Association of Christian publishers (ECPA) Gold Medallion award in 2002.

One of the major points made by Dr. Alcorn, which got my attention, was that there are really two heavens. The first one is called Present Heaven or Paradise. This is where our spirits go upon leaving our bodies, an intermediate stop while waiting for the second Heaven. The second Heaven is where we will spend eternity with God after the 1000-year reign of Jesus on this earth. That location will be this planet. One clue is in the Lord's Prayer, "Thy Kingdom come thy will be done on Earth as it is in Heaven."

The clue that there is an intermediate place called Paradise is in Luke 23: 43. Jesus is hanging on the cross between two condemned criminals. (Luke 23: 39-42) One of the criminals who hung there hurled insults at Him: "Aren't you the Christ? Save yourself and us!" But the other criminal rebuked him. "Don't you fear God," he asked, "since you are under the same sentence? We are punished justly, for we are getting what our deeds deserve, but this man has done nothing wrong." Then he said, "Jesus, remember me when you come into your kingdom." (Verse 43) Jesus answered him, "I TELL YOU THE TRUTH, today you will be with me in Paradise."

How inspiring is the faith of this man who saw the coming glory and not just the current shameful circumstance he was in. In the book "No Wonder They Call Him the Savior", by Max Lucado, he writes about this historical event. "And it also makes me smile to think there is a grinning ex-con walking the golden streets who knows more about grace than a thousand theologians. No one else would have given him a prayer. But in the end, that is all he had. And in the end that is all it took. No wonder they call Him the Savior!"

What is your view of Heaven? Where did you get your information? How many preachers have you heard speak specifically about it? For me, before doing the research for this part of the book, I fell into the category of an overwhelming majority of Americans, according to a poll by the Barna Research Group. I believed there was a Heaven and a Hell, and I got most of my picture of what each would be like from movies, television, conversations with my friends, and some sermons.

Here is how Dr. Alcorn explains the two heavens in his book *Heaven.* "He (Jesus) was referring to the present heaven when speaking to the thief. But why did He call it paradise, and what did it mean? The word paradise comes from the Persian word *pairidaeza*, meaning "a walled park or enclosed garden." It was used to describe the great walled gardens of the Persian King Cyrus's royal palaces. In the Septuagint, the Greek translation of the Old Testament, the Greek word for paradise is used to describe the Garden of Eden (e.g., Genesis 2:8; Ezekiel 28:13). Later, because of the Jewish belief that God would restore Eden, paradise became the word to describe the eternal state of the righteous, and to a lesser extent, the present Heaven.

He further explains why the original Garden of Eden is the present or intermediate Heaven. The clue is "The Tree of Life." In Revelation 2:7, God says, "To him who overcomes, I will give the right to eat from the Tree of Life, which is in the paradise of God." Dr. Alcorn makes a compelling argument that the Tree of Life will also be in the final Heaven. "We are told that after the Fall, God drove the man out; and at the east of the Garden of Eden, He stationed these cherubim and the flaming sword which turns every direction to guard the way to the Tree of Life.

(Genesis 3:24, NASB)." It appears that Eden's Paradise, with the Tree of Life, retained its identity as a physical place but was no longer accessible to mankind. It was guarded by Cherubim, who are residents of Heaven, where God is enthroned between the Cherubim (2 Kings 19:15). Eden was not destroyed. What was destroyed was mankind's ability to live in Eden. In Revelation 22:2, we find evidence that Eden, with the Tree of Life, will be in the final Heaven here on Earth. It says, "On each side of the river stood the Tree of Life, bearing twelve crops of fruit, yielding its fruits every month. And the leaves of the tree are for the healing of the nations."

Other questions covered in the book *Heaven* are:

1. Do people have intermediate bodies in the present Heaven?
2. What can we learn from the story of the rich man and Lazarus? (Luke 16:19-31)
3. What is life like in the present Heaven? (Chapter 7)
4. Do Heaven's inhabitants remember life on earth?
5. Do people in the present Heaven see what is happening on earth?
6. Do people in Heaven pray for those on earth?
7. Can it be Heaven if people are aware of anything bad on earth?

The answer to these questions and much, much more are revealed in Dr. Randy Alcorn's book *Heaven*.

The purpose of this chapter is to make you aware of the different places that wait for you at the end of life. To show you how to get your reservation for Heaven and have your passport ready when the time to go arrives. The time on this current Earth is but a mist, even of those who live to be over 100, in comparison to the time we will spend on the new earth called "Heaven."

I close this chapter with a description of Eternity that I heard in a sermon when I was a teenager and a dream my mother had after serious surgery at age eighty-two before she became a Christian. Let's start with a visual description of Eternity from the sermon as I remember it. Get a visual of a hummingbird. Now imagine that bird picked up one grain of sand on a beach from the Pacific Ocean, traveled across the United States, and deposited that grain of sand on a beach on the Atlantic Ocean. If the bird would continue to do this until all of the sand had been moved from the Pacific Ocean to the Atlantic Ocean, it would be but one day in Eternity. Do you get a sense, as I did, that Eternity is a longer time than we can imagine? So let me ask you "What's in your Future?"

My mother, Betty Marsoobian Kalepgian, had just had major gallbladder surgery and was recovering at home. Mother attended the Armenian Church but at this point in her life had never read the Bible. The Armenian Church did not do Bible studies for individuals. That was left to the priest. This fact makes the story that much more remarkable. This is how I remember her relating the story to me just a few days after her encounter. A cell phone with a video camera would have come in handy at that time.

She began: Sonny (her name for me when she had something serious to talk about), come here and sit down. I

NOTES

NOTES

NOTES

NOTES

ARE YOU READY RELATIONALLY?

When it comes to taking your last God-given breath, the only two things that will matter will be 1) your acceptance of Jesus Christ as your Lord and Savior as was discussed in the previous chapters, and 2) your relationships. Your relationships with your family, your friends, your business associates, coworkers, and your golf, bowling or fishing buddies are what you will be remembered for.

There is a poem read at many funerals about "The Dash." Maybe you have heard it. The dash is that line between the date of your birth and the date of your death. People will say that it represents the life of the departed.

Typically, they don't talk about the size of your stock portfolio, the size of your house, the car you drove, or any of the material things we worry about accumulating during this life. No—the dash represents the impact and influence they had on the lives they touched.

The older I get, the more I think about my dash and what I mean to the people who my life impacted. This section is here to help you think about your dash, so that you might reconcile relationships that have gotten out of line over the years.

You will want to pay close attention to the chapter that discusses the work of Bronnie Wear. She shares her thoughts on the lives of people in her care in the Australian hospice where she works. It's a true revelation.

Because life can end at any time, it's a good idea to make sure you treat everyone with respect and mend old relationships, so you leave with no regrets. Included are my personal experiences when God reached out to me through the Holy Spirit and taught me how to mend my broken relationships

Chapter 7

A REASON—A SEASON—A LIFETIME
(At the end of life, wouldn't it be nice
to be at peace and have no regrets?)

"I'm so sorry that we lost you without giving me a chance to say goodbye. I would give anything for that chance now."
—**Joe Middione**, business owner, at the loss of our friend

R elationships, friendships, partnerships, co-workers, lovers, school friends, church connections, neighbors or people that have come into your life for a reason or a season, we call them "relationships" in this chapter.

In all of these relationships, there are good times, bad times, encouraging words, discouraging words, and sometimes downright anger and disappointment. I have heard, as I'm sure you have, brothers who don't talk to each other, sisters who are estranged, parents who are distant with their children because of disagreements as adults, grandparents denied the chance to talk to their grandchildren. Business partners who started out as best friends but haven't spoken to each other for years over a small disagreement that grew into a mountain of separation.

What a shame it is when we don't get a chance to right the wrongs or correct the mistakes. What a shame it is when you do not say I'm sorry for saying the wrong words that hurt someone, in order to mend a broken relationship before it's too late. You can make contact with an old school buddy, just to catch up on old times, to see how he or she is doing.

Oh yeah, we're going to do that next week. We are going to get together and have lunch or coffee, maybe reminisce, about old times and close the old wounds. Maybe we will do it next week!

Then there's an article in the paper stating that your friend, or your business coworker from years past, has just died. The funeral is on Thursday in his hometown 110 miles away. Suddenly the calendar is clear, and you find time to go to the funeral. Too bad you couldn't find time to have a cup of coffee and share some old memories, just the week before.

Life is a matter of choices. Two events that we always find time for: 1) the funeral of a friend, especially if they die unexpectedly, and 2) a loved one in a hospital emergency room. They are not on the calendar or the "Daily to Do" list, but we make time for them. Why don't we have time to get relationships right before it is time for the memorial service?

Maybe you're lucky, and you hear from somebody that an old business partner is undergoing surgery so you get a chance to visit him in the hospital. You are both able to talk to one another and pray with one another. You talk about how much you appreciated the work and help each gave to the partnership and how much you really love each other. These are the lucky people.

One story that makes this point real occurred a few weeks ago. The person in the story gave me permission to share it. Two men met through business dealings. They were both big sports fans and supporters of Fresno State Football. Their families became so close and spent so much time together that one of each of their children fell in love and married. What seemed like a fairytale story turned into a real life drama, which ended with the two men not speaking, and the families divided.

The part that hurts me was that I considered both very close friends as well.

One of the men was having so many financial and personal issues that in a state of depression he shot himself and did not survive the multiple surgeries to save him. Here is what the other man wrote on Facebook after the memorial service, which was attended by several hundred people.

> *"You see, sometimes in life, you take way too much for granted. It's times like these when you reflect and realize how precious life is, how fast it goes by, and how you should pay attention to the little things. I am thankful for you to remind me of this today."*
> **—Joe Middione**

The other day, there was a story in the paper and on the local TV news about a man, eighty-five years of age, who was taken off life support and died. He was still working every day at his craft of repairing shoes. His customers loved him, his business neighbors adored him, and he loved still being able to work and be of service to others. I'm sure there are many people who would have liked to stop by to thank him and tell him how much they appreciated him. But they never did. I am sure there are plenty of them now saying what a great guy he was. I wonder how many told him that to his face the last time they met.

You see two days ago he was taking a cup of coffee over to his business neighbor, when two young man rushed out of the store, having just robbed it, swinging the door open and knocking the shoe maker down, causing him to hit his head on the ground. He was rushed to the hospital in a coma. He died a short time later after being on life-support from the time he entered the hospital. There were no "Goodbye, I love you" to children, grandchildren, or friends. It all happened in an instant. If he had put one more nail in the shoe before taking the coffee to his friend, he might still be alive today.

We never know what the circumstances are going to be moments before the end of our time on this Earth and the beginning of a completely new world.

While sitting at an intersection on his way to work at an emergency room hospital, a young man was struck by a woman on drugs who ran a red light, killing him instantly. The young man was in his late 20s. Life was just starting for him, his wife, and young baby. The lady that caused the accident was taken to the same emergency room where the victim had been going to work to help others in need, just like her. No goodbyes. No "I'm sorry." No "I'll see you later." Here in the morning, not here at night. Was he ready?

Chapter 8

COMMON REGRETS AT THE END

(What life lessons can we learn from
people who are in hospice care?)

*"You will find as you look back upon your life that the moments
when you have really lived are the moments when you have done
things in the spirit of love."*

—Henry Drummond

An Australian woman named Bronnie Ware was a caregiver for years to many in their final days before dying. She became close to many of them and said that each was able to find his or her own peace before passing on, some sooner than others. Her memoirs about her work with the dying are called *The Top Five Regrets of the Dying: A Life Transformed by the Dearly Departing*. It is available on Amazon. The following is a passage taken from Ware's book.

The number 4 regret among those who were dying was "I wish I had stayed in touch with my friends."

Often they would not truly realize the full benefits of all their friends until their dying weeks, and it was not always possible to track them down. Many had become so caught up in their own lives they had let a golden friendship slip over the years. There were many deep regrets about not giving friendships the time and effort they deserved. Everyone misses their friends when they are dying.

It is common for anyone in a busy lifestyle to let a friendship slip. But when you are faced with your approaching death, the physical details of life fall away. People do want to get their financial affairs in order if possible. But it is not money or status that holds a true importance for them. They want to get things in order more for the benefit of those they love. Usually though, they are too ill and weary to even manage this task. It all comes down to love and relationships in the end. That is all that remains in the final weeks, love and relationships."

People grow a lot when they are faced with their own mortality. I learned never to underestimate someone's capacity for growth. Some changes were phenomenal. Each experienced a variety of emotions, as expected, denial, fear, anger, remorse, more denial and eventually acceptance. Every single patient found their peace before they departed though, every one of them.

When questioned about any regrets they had or anything they would do differently, common themes surfaced again and again. Here are the five most common:

1. I wish I'd had the courage to live a life true to myself, not the life others expected of me.

This was the most common regret of all. When people realize that their lives are almost over and look back clearly on them, it is easy to see how many dreams have gone unfulfilled. Most people had not honored even half of their dreams and had to die knowing that it was due to choices they had made, or not made.

It is very important to try to honor at least some of your dreams along the way. From the moment that you lose your health, it is too late. Health brings a freedom very few realize, until they no longer have it

2. I wish I hadn't worked so hard.

This came from every male patient that I nursed. They missed their children's youth and their partner's companionship. Women also spoke of this regret. But as most were from an older generation, many of the female patients had not been breadwinners. All of the men I nursed deeply regretted spending so much of their lives on the treadmill of a work existence. By simplifying your lifestyle and making conscious choices along the way, it is possible to not need the income that you think you do. And by creating more space in your life, you become happier and more open to new opportunities, ones more suited to your new lifestyle.

3. I wish I'd had the courage to express my feelings.

Many people suppressed their feelings in order to keep peace with others. As a result, they settled for a mediocre existence and never became who they were truly capable of becoming. Many developed illnesses relating to the bitterness and resentment they carried as a result. We cannot control the reactions of others. However, although people may initially react when you change the way you are by speaking honestly, in the end it raises the relationship to a whole new healthier level. Either that or it releases the unhealthy relationship from your life. Either way, you win.

4. (Was listed at beginning of chapter.)
5. I wish that I had let myself be happier.

This is a surprisingly common one. Many did not realize until the end that happiness is a choice. They had stayed stuck in old patterns and habits. The so-called 'comfort' of familiarity overflowed into their emotions, as well as their physical lives. Fear of change had them pretending to others, and to themselves, that they were content. When deep within, they longed to laugh properly and have silliness in their life again. When you are on your deathbed, what others think of you is a long way from your mind. How wonderful to be able to let go and smile again, long before you are dying.

Those who have lived a long time and have had the opportunity to reflect back on their lives have great wisdom to share. One of the things I have become aware of in the last fifteen years since my heart surgery is that life is uncertain. If a little voice tells you to make a call to a friend, do it. It's an old saying, but it's true, "Don't put off for tomorrow what you can do today." Tomorrow may never come, and age and circumstances have little or nothing to do with having more tomorrows.

The following are stories in my life when I needed to either give or ask for forgiveness.

This story starts around October of 1989 when I had accepted the position as a Regional Sales and Marketing Director for the Transamerica Life Insurance Company. I had arranged to sell my agency to a longtime friend in the insurance business who I will call, Ed. We had worked out an agreement where he would, take over my office lease, have access to my brokerage business, and pay me five percent of what the agency would develop over the next three years.

In November 1989, I left Fresno to take my first assignment on the East Coast for Transamerica. In February of 1991, Transamerica discovered that Ed had not relinquished his position as an agent with another insurance company. Transamerica had a rule that said one could not represent Transamerica as a general agent and be an agent for another company. Transamerica then canceled his general agency contract. This resulted in him not completing payment of the lease or being able to fulfill our agreement. Subsequently, I had to pay about two thousand dollars to finish the lease, and I received no future compensation. The Life Insurance agents contracted through my agency were transferred to another agency, which was not obligated to compensate me.

As you can imagine, this caused friction in our relationship as I was expecting him to honor the agreement and at least pay for the lease.

Fast-forward eleven years to March 2001 when I returned to Fresno after having gone through a divorce. Ed became one of my accountability partners as I sought to be reunited with my

Christian brothers in the Christian Business Men's Connection of Fresno. In the fall of 2003, Ed invited me to attend a weekly prayer session with 10-20 men. One morning in 2005, we went through a session of washing each other's feet in a reenactment of what Jesus did for his disciples at the last supper. Ed and I had the opportunity to talk about our business arrangements and asked for an accepted forgiveness in the process of washing each other's feet that Thursday morning. It was a very solemn and cleansing period for both of us. We shook hands and hugged at the conclusion of our time together.

Then about a year and a half later, Ed didn't show up for a Thursday morning prayer time. The morning paper reported a fatal accident on the highway between Fresno and the coast. My friend Ed was driving home alone in his car with his wife and mother-in-law in a car in front of him. An oversized heavy-duty pickup was trying to pass on a two-lane road. His wife was able to swerve out of the way, and my friend Ed and his big Lexus took a direct hit. Ed was on his way to meet the Lord before reaching the hospital. I cried when I heard the news and again at his memorial service. How happy my heart is that we had resolved any issues or conflicts that morning when we washed each other's feet.

His life was cut short. He was in his seventies, seemingly healthy, full of life, a great growing and thriving life insurance business, a beautiful wife, grown children, grandchildren, and it was over in a flash.

This next story shows how important it is to follow your instincts, that small voice in your head, or your gut, whatever you want to call it.

The phone rang early one sunny breezy morning on the island of Oahu. "Hello, Mom, had breakfast yet?"

"Why no, what's up?" Mom said.

"Nothing special, I just thought maybe we could have breakfast before I went off to work. I'll come get you if it's okay."

"Well sure, let me just put something on, and I'll be dressed by the time you get here. Bye."

John hadn't seen his mom for several weeks, and even though they had talked periodically on the phone, it was a rare occasion for them to have breakfast together. John came by, picked up his mom, and they went to the restaurant. They talked about the kids, about life in general, as well as the family plans. It was a nice breakfast and visit between a mother and her only son. John took his mom home.

"Thanks mom that was great."

"Yeah it was, John. Let's do it again."

"Okay, will talk to you later. Love you."

"Love you, too, John."

John went down the hill and headed off to work. Within the next hour, John was struck by a car and was off to see the Lord, who he loved. He was on his motor scooter, the kind that many people ride in Hawaii. This young man, full of life, left behind his mom and four daughters, from age 16 to 26.

Is it strange that mom and son would have breakfast? NO. What is strange is that he would pick this morning, on a whim, to call his mom to have breakfast. There are no accidents in the universe, and I believe God set it up. What a blessing that they had that breakfast. Mom could have said that I too tired or she would rather do it tomorrow. Something inside him said, "Call and ask Mom to go for breakfast." They're both thankful that he listened to the inner voice and acted upon what he knew was the right thing to do.

I learned of the story because I was listening to my inner voice to make a call to Barbara, the "MOM". We have been friends since high school days. Because of an unfortunate situation, a misunderstanding, she had not spoken to me in over twelve years. My inner voice told me to call and apologize for anything that I had said or done that caused us to not be connected as we were for so many years. Not knowing what to expect on the other end of the line, I was thrilled when our conversation lasted for over 45 minutes. With some tears on my part at the beginning, I asked for and received her forgiveness. This allowed us to then move on in the conversation and not dwell on whatever the problem had been. It just wasn't important anymore.

I was thrilled to hear my friend's voice and to connect with her again, to listen to the story of how she had lost her son. We then went on to talk about the grandchildren, and yes, she even has a great-grandchild. John was her only son, and these children are now the only immediate family she has left.

I'll sleep better tonight, and I hope she does as well, knowing that we reconnected. I gave her my new phone number and told to call whenever she felt like it. I said that I would do the same. "Goodbye, my friend, I love you," I said. "Me, too," she said. What a great day! Sure was good to take my own advice about relationships and healing wounds before it's too late.

One last story that makes the point of this chapter in such a way I had to add it. This is from Pastor David Jeremiah's daily devotional on December 12, 2014. "Last February, John Allen, a British lawyer living in Holland, smiled across the supper table at his wife and three sons, ages eight to fourteen. Someone snapped a picture. They were happy. A family vacation to Indonesia was in the works.

Five months later the five Allen's boarded Malaysia Airlines Flight MH17, but somewhere over Ukraine the plane was blown out of the sky. The whole family perished in an instant, along with their fellow passengers. We can't comprehend the evil and calamity in the world. Such tragedies deeply upset and depress us, but they also represent a poignant reminder. Take every opportunity to cherish your loved ones. If you're peeved with a family member, forgive them. If you have neglected them, give them a call. If you have rebelled against your dad or mom, go home with the humble attitude of a repentant prodigal. If you have been tense with your kids, give them an extra hug. If you live far away, work harder to stay in touch. Whatever it takes, take care of your family as well as you can. It is at the core of God's plan and provision for the world."

The next section deals with leaving a legacy and financial support for the loved ones left behind.

Section II

RELATIONSHIPS

NOTES:

Did a few people come to mind you want to reach out too? Use these pages to write their names down so you can go back and contact them.

NOTES

NOTES

NOTES

NOTES

ARE YOU READY FINANCIALLY?

In the first two sections, you were dealing with subjects that impacted you directly. They were where you are going after this world, and how you are going to feel about relationships and people you served while you were here.

Being ready financially is your responsibility, and you must make the decisions. However, the consequences of your decisions will impact people you love and the way they live their lives once you are gone. Once you're dead, you are dead a long, long time. You will not be coming back to be of any help.

This section will give you practical information and formulas to help you in your decision-making. It pulls from my three decades in the life insurance profession and my relationships with others concerning with whether you are ready financially.

In the capitalistic society we live in, the accumulation of wealth and material possessions are the way most people measure success. In the proper context, this is good. A business that doesn't make a profit will soon stop being a business. A family that doesn't watch how they spend will find themselves either deep in debt or worse—homeless. So the accumulation of wealth and material possessions is not wrong in and of itself. It is the importance placed on the value of that accumulation when measuring the contributions You made in your life. As we asked earlier, what will be in your "DASH."

The status in which you leave your loved ones will also be a measure of your success in life. The Federal Government currently says you can pass on to your loved ones around five million dollars tax-free. A life insurance contract is the cheapest way to leverage this gift. In a way, if you don't leave at least this much, people might think that you took it with you.

This section explains how this works and other tips on using the Federal tax codes, as well as using life insurance to make a positive impact on the lives of the people you love, even if you are not coming back and are going to be dead a long, long time.

Chapter 9

LEAVE A LEGACY

(Being remembered for what you have done
to make life easier for those left behind)

"What you give away you keep forever, what you keep you lose."
—Anonymous

The value of a life lived well will be based on how much of yourself is given away. In the end, you will not be judged by the things that you accumulated, the business you built, or the financial size of your estate.

The next time you are at a funeral, listen carefully to the eulogy. Is it about the size and location of the house they lived in, the car they drove, their stock portfolio? No! It is about the lives they touched, the service they gave to others, how connected they were to their family, and what their spiritual base was. Also take a look around you, who is in attendance? Family only, business associates, civic leaders, friends? The people who attend your memorial service will say a lot about how you lived your life.

Years ago at a funeral for a man in his late 40's who lost his life in a robbery attempt, my mother made a comment to me as we were leaving the services. "Arsen, who was this man, and why was he so respected?"

"Why do you ask that, Mom? You knew him."

"Look around at all the different kinds of people who are here. There are men in business suits. There are others who look like they're homeless, politicians, some women who look like prostitutes. You have rich and poor, you have old and young, black and white. This man was no ordinary person, and he was very well liked. He surely touched a lot of lives."

This man, who was a close acquaintance of mine, served the community as a volunteer youth sports coach, was a devoted family man, and was involved in local politics but wasn't a politician. He owned a local bar and had no spiritual life that I was aware of. His funeral service is still the largest attended in that Holy Trinity Armenian Apostolic Church, well over 1,000 people. I cannot remember anything said about him during the service, but my mother's comments afterward spoke volumes about him.

When one hears the term "legacy," it usually brings thoughts of a wealthy individual leaving lots of money to heirs and charities. However, you don't have to be a millionaire to leave a legacy. In fact, we all leave a legacy. The question is what is it going to be? How you live and die becomes your legacy.

In the late 60s and early 70s during the rise of motivational speakers, one of the best known was a man named Jim Rohn.

When he was a speaker in Fresno, I had the privilege of meeting him and became a student of his by purchasing and studying his material. One of the many ideas he taught was on a legacy you could leave that would be remembered long after the money was gone and material things were broken or lost.

Was it how to set up a trust, or the process of transferring wealth, or the expensive valuables? NO! It was so different, so basic, that I never forgot it. In fact, I have been trying to make sure I leave these three things to my family. These three things can be done by everyone regardless of any financial status in life. It is what I call a true "Legacy."

1. Leave a journal of your thoughts and ideas. (Let them know what you thought and believed in the moment.)
2. Leave a library of books and recordings of great ideas, philosophies and religions. (Let them know what you read to form your personality and belief system.)
3. Leave your loved ones pictures of the people and places that touched your life. It only takes a second to capture the moment. With a camera on every smartphone, this is so much easier than when Mr. Rohn was advocating for it.

There you have it, journal, library, and pictures are a true legacy that everyone can, and should, leave.

These may be the things our loved ones remember, but they are not what society will use to help pay the bills. Money is important in all the areas where only money can be used.

Money is not the root of all evil. The misuse of it can cause evil. When Jesus was asked about paying taxes, he answered by asking whose face was on the coin? It was Caesar. "Give to Caesar what is Caesar's and to God what is God's."

Leaving our loved ones without any debt to pay and the financial means to have a secure and meaningful life is important. That's why the next chapter covers the different programs and ideas for your consideration while you are still healthy enough to take advantage of them.

Chapter 10

PROTECTING THOSE LEFT BEHIND
(How to cheat death and have control from the grave)

"Life Insurance is protecting those you love from those you owe."
—**Arsen S. Marsoobian**, CLU

L et's start at the beginning. Life is expensive. When someone dies, there is a shock, a funeral, a period of grieving, incredible adjustments that must be made, but then, *life goes on*. Yes, it's a cliché, but like many clichés, the reason it's said so often is that there is great truth in it. No matter how much we were loved (or are still loved), no matter how big a part of their lives we were, our death is not the end for our loved ones. After an appropriate time of grieving, delaying the time when our family picks up and continues their lives is not good for them, nor does it help anyone else.

There are many ways to protect those left behind from financial disaster. These include a savings account, stock market portfolio, pension plans, individual retirement accounts (IRAs), business interests, stocks from privately held companies, real estate holdings, and life insurance policies. How these assets are owned "legally" determines the manner in which they will be transferred, to whom they will be transferred, and the cost associated with that transfer. (Note: Only life insurance programs are covered, as this is my area of expertise.)

It is not my intention to give legal or financial advice. Please look at your own circumstances and seek professional advice as to what is best for you and your family. I have been a life insurance salesman and an executive for some of the largest life insurance companies in the world. I've dedicated half my life to its study and practice. This information is a simple and brief overview of how life insurance works and how you can use its power to your advantage.

Using life insurance wisely satisfies a natural human desire to have an impact from the grave. We want to be remembered well. We want to provide even when we are gone. It is a natural human impulse—and a good one—that we want to be a blessing while we are here. With life insurance, we can do it even after we're gone.

However, it takes planning because death is a show with no dress rehearsal. It is a game where you can't make adjustments at halftime. There are no second shots. When you are six feet under, you are in no position to renegotiate. Whether you are directing your greatest victory or making your worst mistake, it will be your last. It will be your final victory or your concluding blunder.

If this all sounds a little dramatic, I can tell you it's not. There are heartwarming stories of families and loved ones, even charities, being well provided for, and horror stories of children, elderly parents and spouses falling on tough times following the death and sometimes an untimely, unanticipated death, of a loved one. All these scenarios play out every day. How you handle them in death and in life will depend on what you know and how you act concerning life insurance.

When I began my career selling life insurance, I would typically give long-winded and confusing answers to the question, "Why should I buy life insurance?" However, after years of thought and helping many clients, I was able to create a solid accurate answer. Just eight words: *"Protecting those you love from those you owe."*

When the people we love and leave behind reach this point, you can bet they'll rediscover this truth: life is expensive. Knowing this and contemplating what they will face as they continue their lives, the question is, "How do we provide for them," or in other words, "How do we protect them from expenses they'll be faced with in our absence?"

Before we go any further into this conversation, here is an important note. As someone who has guided hundreds of people through the process of answering this question, I understand how challenging it is. It requires us to contemplate our mortality and think about that seriously enough to make an intelligent plan, and it is not easy. That's why many of my clients have concluded it's the most responsible and adult thing they have ever done. I agree. My congratulations to you for reaching this point. Many never do and while I would like to say, "They live to regret it," the truth is the regrets come after they are no longer alive, and they are borne by those whom they said that they loved. True love has many qualities, and my business has been helping people see that love and foresight rank high among them. It has been my privilege to serve many families with their life insurance needs. I now hope to serve you, by helping you access these qualities from within your own character, and do great and loving deeds with them. To help you understand how life insurance works and where it fits in your plans.

My father died in 1950 at the age of fifty-five with no life insurance. My mother had to sell everything to pay off his debts and to continue with her life alone, raising a rebellious 15-year-old boy. Fortunately, less than a year later, she married a wonderful man, which helped matters out financially and brought stability to the house. However, many widows find themselves marrying less than stellar men because of their financial needs and not for the individual's character or love between them. I can tell you that this is an unfortunate situation that can be avoided with the proper amount of life insurance coverage.

The expenses a family faces that can be lessened or eliminated by life insurance can be broken down into two categories: those associated directly with the death of a loved one ("immediate"), and those that take into account the people who we love and how they are going to live into the future ("ongoing"). There are many fact-finding documents that a qualified life insurance agent will use to help you come to the right number.

When considering your life insurance purchase make the best estimate possible regarding how much money your loved ones will need to pay off debts and pay for ongoing expenses in your absence. These are listed later in this chapter. Then look at all the other resources available to them, which were listed above. Then choose an amount of life insurance that will comfortably make up the difference.

Don't tackle this task on your own. Make as good an estimate as you can and then consult a professional life insurance salesperson as well as your accountant and perhaps an estate tax attorney when making your final decision. Remember that unexpected needs tend to occur more often than unexpected sources of income.

In reality, many of the expenses will be incurred years or decades into the future, making estimates even harder to calculate. Still, it's important to have an awareness of what these future expenses might be. One way of estimating the appropriate amount of life insurance to buy, and the one your life insurance agent will probably use, is called "Human Life Value" or HLV.

Before we go any further, here is a note. Some people are sensitive about the term "Human Life Value" because it sounds like it means someone is deciding what you are worth as a human being. This is not what it means at all. Here is what it actually means. HLV takes your current annual income and multiplies that by the number of years you estimate you will continue to work, customarily to age 66. It does not account for increases in pay you are likely to receive. That number is your HLV, and its purpose is to be a gauge for how much life insurance you need to replace your lost income to your loved ones. Obviously, this is a large amount of money. How are you supposed to make sense of such a large number, or pay for that large of a policy? However, you need to find a way to account for replacing such a large amount of money if you are not around to earn it each month. It makes sense to account for all possible sources of income available to reduce this large number. The gap left between these two numbers is a reasonable place for your life insurance policy to start.

You can use this formula to figure your HLV.

Your current age _____ minus age you want to stop working _____ = number of earning years left _____.

The number of earning years left _____ multiplied by your annual earnings $_____ = your personal HLV $_____.

For instance, if you are 30 years old and earning $50,000 per year, and you estimate you will work until you are 65, your HLV would be 35 times $50,000, or $1,750,000 not accounting for increases in pay you will earn along the way.

Your current age __30__ minus age you want to stop working __65__ = number of earning years left __35__.

The number of earning years left __35____ multiplied by your annual earnings $_50,000_ = your personal HLV $_1,750,000_.

Now this could be a very large number, and it's hard to see how you could afford to pay for this much protection. So I help my clients by asking them if the surviving spouse has any of these income options.

Six possibilities of income to surviving loved ones:

The surviving spouse's career or job.

- Your retirement benefits such as a pension or a 401K.
- Stock Dividends.

- An ongoing interest in or sale of a business.
- Real estate investments other than family home.
- Government programs, i.e. Social Security, or welfare

Then the next two questions you should answer are:

1. How important is it to you that the people you love be able to afford the things they want and need?
2. How much can you afford per month to protect those you love and give them the life they want even if you're not here to provide it?

The answer to these two questions will determine how much you can cheat death by reaching out from the grave and having a major impact on the lives of the living.

Countless people have cheated death, so to speak, and it is a powerful thing, a generous thing, and a loving thing. The way you can do this with life insurance is by leaving detailed instructions on the distribution of the money from the policy. You have the right to decide not only whom you want to receive it, but the manner they receive it and how they can use the money. Depending on how complicated your situation is you may want to seek out an estate planning attorney to get a trust established to direct the use of the money.

You can alleviate suffering, relieve anxiety, lift unfair and unmanageable burdens, and bring ease to situations that would otherwise be harsh and difficult, if not impossible. You can spare the older people you leave behind from pain and heartache, and you can provide the younger ones with the opportunity and freedom that lets them create lives and experiences far beyond what they could have done without your assistance. You can be a hero, a champion, a protector, a sage, and a source of wisdom and light, or you can simply be gone, absent and finished.

In the next chapter, we will cover specific expenses at time of death and how you can provide income to your loved ones long after you are gone.

Chapter 11

PROVIDING FROM THE GRAVE

(Can you cheat death by making
an impact on people still living?)

*"Our children are our only hope for the future, but we are their
only hope for their present and their future."*
—**Zig Ziglar**, personal development speaker and author

I n my book, *DON'T DIE F: 3 Essential Truths For a Fulfilled and
Happy Life (Regardless of Your Age)*, I make a point regarding
immortality and a way to achieve it, "To do something with
your life that will live on in the lives of others long after you
are gone." Life insurance is a way to do that by providing the
security to help other people do good and important things after
you are no longer in this life.

Reaching out from beyond the grave by using life insurance
begins with anticipating and handling expenses for people in a
way that makes their lives better. I am not talking about paying
for things that they rightly should pay for themselves. These

expenses are not anticipated and come crashing down on your loved ones. Without some form of help, these expenses typically set them back several steps on the pathway of recovery from their loss.

Let's look at some of these and explore how, with proper planning, you can be a force for good in the world long after you are gone.

As I stated earlier, there are immediate expenses that set people back at time of death. Let's take a look at what those expenses are.

Funeral:

According to the National Funeral Directors Association, the average funeral in the U.S. costs about $8,000. Unless you've carefully planned your own funeral, there are numerous decisions that will need to be made and most of them amount to shopping: from caskets, to limos, to flowers, to a catered lunch. These are all choices that cannot wait. In the best of circumstances, people find them uncomfortable. They are even more difficult when price and how they are going to be paid for are weighing heavy on the mind. Knowing funds are in place to take care of these expenses relieves one of the greatest sources of anxiety at a time when a huge amount of stress is unavoidable.

If you are someone who cares about how people think of you, then you should know that these are the moments when people will think about you and memories will be shaped. The two dominant emotions in these circumstances are gratitude and regret, and it is usually one or the other. Better to be saying, "I'm glad I did," not "I wish I had."

Probate:

Probate means the official proving of a will as authentic and valid in a court of law. If you've ever packed up your house to move, or taken on a big spring cleaning project you have probably realized that you've accumulated more stuff than you thought. That's how it is with an "estate," meaning, all the property of a deceased person. Most of the time there is more that needs to be handled than you would think and handling it costs money.

When an estate goes through probate, attorneys, appraisers, executors, various others and the court itself, usually all receive fees. Assessments vary state-by-state and case-by-case, but as a rough example, let's look at an estate in California that consists of no other property except a house valued at $300,000. Such an estate would cost $10,000-$15,000 to take through probate. If the estate does not also contain that amount of dollars in cash, where does that money come from?

When an estate has value but it doesn't have much cash, the assets have to be sold to pay off the costs of processing the estate, whether the inheritors want to sell them or not. Most of the time, people want to keep the things they inherit. Sometimes people are living in the homes they inherit and don't want to move. Furniture, antiques, artwork and collectibles often have sentimental value and are things people would never want to part with. Then at other times, market conditions favor holding onto them.

Court files are full of stories of family members that have inherited very valuable assets but no cash, and consequently, they had to sell the assets.

Remember, the IRS doesn't take credit cards. They want one thing: cash! And they want it within nine months of your death. You may have heard of cases when the deceased was a famous person, and the family had to sell off assets to pay estate taxes. We all assume famous people are rich and can afford to pay their tax bills, but in many cases, famous or not, people die wealthy but with no cash. Here is an example of what happens more times than you can believe.

One of the most famous actors who died in 2013, James Gandolfini, left his family in a catastrophic situation. "It's a nightmare from a tax standpoint," said William Zabel, who reviewed the document at the request of The New York Daily News. His family will have to start selling off his property and liquidating his assets soon in order to pay the tab since it's unlikely the actor had tens of millions of dollars in cash on hand. "The government doesn't accept the fact that it's difficult to come up with the money you owe," said the lawyer, who has represented the likes of billionaire George Soros and "King of All Media" Howard Stern. Gandolfini died with an estate worth an estimated $70 million. Gandolfini's will left about 80 percent of his estate unprotected against estate taxes, with rates that will add up to about 55 percent when you consider both the federal and state portions. That leaves just $31,500,000 to be distributed as Gandolfini wished. This means that his widow, to whom he left 20% of the estate, will receive about $6,300,000 after the will is settled and taxes are paid. His son, Michael received the proceeds of a $7 million life insurance policy within two weeks and isn't subject to estate tax nor affected by the will issues.

Here are just a few other famous people who died only to leave their families with huge tax problems: artist Thomas Kinkade, baseball player Ted Williams, entertainers Ray Charles and Whitney Houston, and business mogul, John D. Rockefeller. Wealth or fame is no indication that a person had good financial planning advice.

The key to financial success is forethought, thinking ahead, planning wisely and executing your plan. All the fame in the world does not guarantee you will have financial success. In the end, it is better for inheritors to have the choice to sell or keep the things that are "willed" to them. In order to make this choice, they need cash. Nothing provides cash quicker, or at a lower cost when it is needed, more than life insurance does.

Attorney's Fees:

In some states, attorney fees for handling probate cases are set by law, and in other states, they are not. Either way, a good lawyer never comes cheap. When you die, your loved ones may need a lawyer, and that lawyer will have to be paid. An established life insurance policy in force at the time of death could avoid this expense.

Estate Taxes:

When you die, there is a federal tax on your estate. This is called an "estate tax." Some people call it a "death tax." There is a popular saying that goes, "No one should have to visit the undertaker and the tax assessor on the same day." More on that in a moment!

When calculating what you owe in estate taxes, start by counting the net value of everything you own. Remember, a tax is levied on every dollar over a certain amount. The amount that is not taxed is called your "exemption." As of this writing, the exemption for federal estate taxes is $5,250,000, and the balance of the estate is taxed at 40 percent.

Many people think they don't have to worry about the estate tax because they are not worth five million dollars, but here are two important points to consider:

The total amount of your estate can add up very quickly especially if you own a business. Other assets include your home and other real estates, all your savings and investments, money in retirement accounts, expensive toys like a boat, motorcycle or RV, any collections like stamps, coins, sports memorabilia and art. The proceeds from a life insurance contract are added to the estate for taxable calculations if the policy owner is also the insured. However, a good agent should be able to structure your policy to avoid having to pay estate taxes on the money. The point is: the government will count everything.

ii. The estate tax exemption has changed many times in recent years, and most of the time it has increased. However, lowering it is frequently discussed, especially as a means of raising money when the government is struggling. Assuming you will not need cash to pay taxes on your estate is not the best long-term planning. It is true that you currently do not have to pay estate taxes on assets that pass between spouses; however, this could change.

Final Medical Expenses:

Health care is very often an enormous drain on assets near the end of life. Here is a frequent scenario. A person thinks they have plenty of money to cover all their debts and expenses, and they anticipate leaving their loved ones a good amount of money. Then they get sick!

Some estimates show that one-third of all the money we spend on healthcare during our lives is spent in the final years of life. It's not uncommon to spend vast sums on an illness from which we will recover. Hospital patients who enter intensive care in the final month of life, for instance, can expect to rack up more than $35,000 in charges in less than a week.

The lesson is that you might think you have enough cash to cover costs associated with the end of your life, but an illness, even a brief one, can be so expensive that it wipes out whatever you've put aside. However, many life insurance contracts now will allow you to take a portion of the death benefit to cover end-of-life medical needs. Some are having long-term care benefits built into their policies. This feature is becoming more popular among all life insurance companies. You may want to ask your agent about these policies.

Long-Term care:

Another expense that rapidly depletes savings and assets near the end of life is long-term health care. The average cost of a nursing home is about $70,000 per year, but it can be much more depending on where you live and the type of care you need and want. One study showed that half of all nursing home residents are broke after six months of residency. Let's assume the length of stay before death is three years. In-home healthcare can be even more expensive. The average cost for round-the-clock care is more than $13,000 per month. You'll pay an average of $20 per hour for aid in the home, and much more for nursing care. Long-term care policies are a separate matter from life insurance. The pros and cons of this kind of policy is a subject you will want your life insurance agent to explain. If you are under age 70, you should also ask about the newest policies where companies are combining life insurance and long-term care as riders.

Medicaid:

Medicaid is a state-administered program that helps pay the medical expenses of people who cannot afford them. If Medicaid pays any of your medical bills before your death, the State will be first in line to be reimbursed for the cost of care to the extent that your estate has any assets at all. Here is a common scenario. If you become ill and can't afford to pay your medical bills, but you own a home, Medicaid will not require you to sell it, and they will step in and help with your bills.

However, after you die, and your house becomes part of your estate, Medicaid will want to be reimbursed, and the house would have to be sold to pay that reimbursement. This is another instance when not having cash to pay bills can play havoc with the hopes and plans you want to leave your loved ones. Check with your agent for the rules in your state. This is my experience in California.

Immediate Lost Wages:

Before a serious illness ends a life, it brings a halt to many other things as well, including work and the ability to earn a living. The immediate loss of wages by the surviving spouse is another financial factor that has to be accounted for when anticipating costs that accumulate at the end of life. It is a difficult but often necessary situation for a grieving spouse to take time off from work. However, if they are in a position that requires them to return to work immediately or be fired, money from a life insurance policy can bridge this gap.

One of my clients, whom I will call Dick and Jane, were in their late thirties when I was first referred to them. Dick took out a $250,000 term policy at Jane's objection thinking it was too expensive. Dick was in good health and was issued a Preferred Policy. About three years later, Dick called and wanted more coverage. This time, he bought a permanent plan for an additional $150,000. He was also given a Preferred Rating. They had three growing teenage children so Jane went back to work to fill in the financial gaps. Dick was a sole business owner in the construction field.

A year later, Dick started having headaches that wouldn't go away. During a visit to the doctor, Dick was diagnosed with an inoperable brain tumor. The deadly disease took a little more than eighteen months to finally take his life. During this time, particularly in the last six months, Jane did all she could to keep her job, take care of her dying husband, and raise three teenage children. When Dick died at age forty-three, it was a hard blow to Jane even though it was expected. Within a week of the funeral, her employer called to inform her that she was needed back at work the following week. She was too valuable to the company for her to be gone much longer.

Dick's death brought with it many more problems than anyone had anticipated. It was a very emotional time for the children, and their mom was doing all she could to work through those issues. The delivering of the life insurance money within the two-week period of time was one of the most satisfying payments I ever delivered. Jane had enough money to quit her job and be at home for her children. She made sure they received the education and life both she and Dick wanted them to have. Jane returned to work a few years later on her terms.

Travel:

When someone dies close to home and is laid to rest in the same town, and all his loved ones live nearby, there may not be any travel expenses associated with the end of his or her life. However, that isn't the case for many people or families today. Retirees want to be buried where they lived most of their lives. Siblings and other family members come from far and wide. All the traveling has to be hastily arranged, and none of it is cheap. The funds to pay for airfare, lodging, meals and everything associated with hosting a group of travelers may or may not be available, causing yet another strain on an already stressed out family.

In all these circumstances, a ready and abundant source of cash can enable an extended family to meet a plethora of sudden and significant expenses with confidence and ease so that they can gather, mourn, remember, take stock of their lives individually and together, reflect with gratitude for the life of the departed and for each other, and move on with grace and joy. Not having those funds can lead to a very different experience, less harmonious, more anxious, less certain, more disjointed, and with less opportunity for positive remembrances.

Now let's look at the ongoing and future expenses needed.

Monthly Income:
After the death of a family provider, the total monthly costs will drop by about 30 percent. The provider was probably earning far more than 30 percent of the family's income. When you are considering how your family would go forward in a situation like this, there are a number of ongoing and future expenses you should be aware of. One initial question is: Are you willing for your family to have to lower their standard of living because of your death, and if so, by how much?

Housing:
Mortgage or rent is usually a family's largest and most important monthly expense. The last thing a widow or widower, who is suddenly a single parent, wants to be faced with is having to find a new home and moving. The fact that you're downscaling to a less expensive house and neighborhood doesn't help matters. Adding all that stress to the sorrowful load the newly single parent is already carrying is a cruel blow to their well-being, and could be a threat to the person's health.

I've sold countless life insurance policies to spouses and parents whose number one concern was paying off the house. They wanted to know that if they could not be there to work and pay the mortgage that their spouse and kids could go on living in the same home. I've always felt it was the responsible and necessary thing to do.

Childcare:
Whether it is the mother or the father who suffers an untimely passing, when one parent dies, it places an incredible childcare burden on the surviving parent. In instances of divorce, one parent usually winds up with the majority of childcare responsibilities, but the parent making the lesser contribution still pitches in to some extent. In cases of premature death, the departing parent is completely absent. No weekends, no holidays, no summer vacations, nothing. Even the death of a parent when the parents are already divorced means a loss that is emotional, substantive, and complete. All these situations produce an incredible childcare burden.

When a stay-at-home parent dies, the surviving parent has to replace 100 hours of childcare or more, and while close relatives may be willing to help temporarily, in the long run, most of those hours will wind up being covered by people you will have to pay. When the departing parent is the one who mainly works outside the home, the stay-at-home parent, or the working parent who has typically handled most of the domestic duties, will probably have to increase his or her working hours. Whatever the case, most of the time it calls for paying more childcare, and those costs will be at least hundreds and possibly thousands of dollars per month.

A little known strategy is to have benefits structured so that these costs can be paid on a monthly basis for a set period of time, giving you control over the well-being of your family for years after you are gone

Tuition and Education:

College tuition is rising at a rate close to 5 percent per year, and is consistently double the rate of inflation. Parents typically save for college as their children grow and, hopefully, the parents' earnings increase. The best way to compensate when a child loses a parent is to invest a lump sum and let it grow as the child matures, but you need to have that money available right away.

Business Expenses:

There are more than five million businesses in the United States with 100 or fewer employees. You can bet that the owners are integral to the success and the ongoing operation of every one of those businesses, and when one of them suffers an untimely death, the business will immediately face unexpected challenges. When the business is family owned, and that's true in many cases, keeping the business running smoothly is crucial to the well-being of the family of the deceased.

Meanwhile, as any small business owner can tell you, every employee represents a family that is also dependent on the business's continuing success. If you own a business, the possibility that you would die, however unlikely and remote, is nothing to deny. Banks, the IRS, and other creditors may consist of individuals who are sympathetic when there is a sudden death, but that doesn't change the facts about financial obligations. It doesn't change one iota how those institutions will behave when their interests are at stake.

Look at what happened with the housing crisis of 2008. As recently as 2012, there were still nearly one-third of American homeowners underwater! With 40 million homeowners in all, when you read the reporting on the crisis you can find words like "foreclosure" and "eviction," but you won't find words like "compassion" or "understanding" or "forgiveness."

It's not uncommon for a business to need a ready source of cash that it can borrow from when there is a disruption among the owners. Good luck getting a loan from a bank when the continuity of your business is in question. No one will care, at least not in terms of how they do business with you, or that your difficulty is being caused by a sad and untimely death.

I think you can see now, it is expensive if death comes suddenly or after a long illness. Please be prepared.

Section III

FINANCIALLY

NOTES:

Leaving A Legacy requires some personal soul searching for some. Use these pages to make notes of people who are important to you. How do you want them to remember you? Maybe use the space to do some personal math from formulas in the section.

NOTES

NOTES

NOTES

NOTES

NOTES

ARE YOU READY? ONE LAST TIME

For the Last Heartbeat

Chapter 12

THE LAST WORD

(Summary of the points made to get you ready,
Spiritually, Relationally, and Financially)

*"Remember, you can earn more money, but when time is spent it
is gone forever."*

—**Zig Ziglar**, personal development speaker, author

I f you have reached this point in the book, you should now understand and believe the quote we opened with: "You never truly start to live until you are no longer afraid to die." Living each day with the assurance of where your soul will spend Eternity gives you a sense of freedom like nothing else. The first few chapters covered this subject.

You may recall the story of my mother's dream, then her accepting the truth of who Jesus is. The rest of that story was what happened at her funeral. Remember, my mother went to church and was reading the Bible I had purchased for her. It was also a time in my life when I had reconnected with my faith in

Jesus. I was learning and reading the Bible with understanding for the first time in my life.

When Mother passed, she was to have her service in her home church, Holy Trinity Armenian Apostolic Church of Fresno. She had served and worshiped there for over sixty years. There was no question that this was where she wanted her funeral service to be held.

However, wanting to have her faith in Christ acknowledged, I asked the pastor from Evangelical Free Church of Fresno to give the eulogy and speak. The particulars were worked out between the clergy, and the service was one of celebration. I can remember telling myself not to smile at the graveside service. Many of my mother's Armenian friends would not understand my joy of knowing that she was already united with Jesus in Paradise.

At age 88, there was no more pain or suffering. This time she would be welcomed home because her name was written in one of those big books on a table with a clergy behind it. I know without any doubt, Betty Marsoobian Kalepgian's name was written in the Book of Life.

Have you ever been to a funeral service, and there was no mention of Jesus? Maybe Jesus, heaven, or falling asleep were mentioned or even preached, but when family and friends talked about the departed, there was no evidence that they knew or had accepted Jesus?

I have, and they are in stark contrast to feelings I just described at my mother's funeral. They are sad times. The worst times were when I had an opportunity to share the story, but couldn't because I didn't know the Bible well enough to find the answers.

I hope that sharing the story of Nicodemus will help you either personally come to faith in Jesus, or help you share the good news with a loved one or friend before it is too late.

In the chapter "A Reason—A Season—A Lifetime," we covered the importance of solving the hurts and healing the broken relationships before it's too late.

People will come into of our lives throughout our lives. Some are for a particular reason. They help you get over a problem, introduce you to a doctor for a second opinion that saves your life, or any number of reasons. These are short periods of hours, days, weeks, maybe a month or two. I have had a lot of them in my 80 plus years.

One was a woman who came into my life because my third wife Susie met her son at the swimming pool in our apartment complex. We were neighbors for a short time, kept in contact for a while, but lost track for about five years. She is an international journalist and actor by profession. Her name is Malgosia Gibble, and I am aware that she appeared in the movie "Schindler's List" and the TV series "ER." We had a chance meeting and reconnection sometime before my first heart surgery. During Thanksgiving dinner at our home, I mentioned the failure of the surgery and having to wait a dangerous year before anything could be done. "If I can get you into doctors at UCLA Medical Center, would you go for a second opinion," she asked.

"Yes" came my answer. Less than a month later, I would be getting ready for my lifesaving second open heart surgery at UCLA Medical Center, by one of only five doctors in the world who could perform that surgery that soon. It's been sixteen years, and I have not talked or seen that lady since.

Then comes those people that are with you for a season, a period of time from months to years. The experience can be good or bad, or a little of both. There are a few of these people in my life as well. If you take a few minutes to close your eyes, I bet you can think of several people in this category and the one before.

I believe there are no accidents in the Universe. God has us meet the people we need to meet, and when we need to meet them. They help him do His work in our lives. Some call them guardian angels. Maybe you have been one yourself. One such case for me was the chance meeting of a lady by the name of Lynn Lambrecht. We met at a two-day seminar in Los Angeles in 2011. She is the author of *The Living Planner* ©. This is what she says about her book, *The Living Planner* was written as a resource guide for immediate use throughout America. What is your readiness level? Have you sorted out your life so that your loved ones are aware and protected when you transition from life?

Protect Your Assets, Honor Their Wishes... Planning for life includes planning for death. Dealing with end of life details requiring immediate attention can take away from the grief you feel after someone dies. This resource guide includes three easy to use action sheets for individual completion: Pre-Planning, After a Loss, and Ongoing Follow-up.

I hadn't found resources to assist me with the practical matters of death when I needed to take care of important details for my family/friends, thus I wrote one. It is written as an overview and contains a tremendous amount of information, packed in a short resource guide. My hope is that people will approach this topic while fully engaged in living, thus participating fully in the process and assisting loved ones, before it's needed.

In the introduction of her e-book on Kindle, *Death of a Loved One*, she covers what the underlying theme for this book is.

By nature, people avoid issues that are difficult, distasteful, or simply not pressing. There is no easy way to approach the subject of death. Practical matters in preparation for death may be the last item on your to-do list, but there will come a time when you are called to face the reality of dealing with death.

This reality struck me personally when my friend Jim died suddenly of a heart attack. I again faced the matter of death when my father, who was a two-time cancer survivor, had two heart failures in two months. His Alzheimer's had progressed rapidly, and he was no longer able to care for himself. He died within three weeks of entering a nursing home. I also bore witness to others handling the sudden deaths of loved ones during my career in the aviation industry. As an emergency response team member, I was called to work with families after three fatal incidents.

Each of us has had unique and personal experiences involving death. While most of us enter into the world within a period of nine months, our exit from this world is unpredictable. Death may be sudden and unexpected or follow a prolonged illness. In either event, I pose these questions: Are your affairs in order? Have you prepared for death?

If you go to her website TheLivingPlanner.com, you can get this book with all the wonderful planning ideas, for before, at time of death, and after death period. You will also get excellent worksheets and forms to help you get yourself and your loved ones organized.

Another resource I found for the "how to" part of this subject is by a friend who lives here in Fresno, California. His name is Rick Cox, and the name of his consulting company is "Care Services." His company motto is "Trusted Funeral Coordinating & Guidance." Check it out on Facebook, "Care Services Central Valley CA." or email him at rcdc08@gmail.com.

Are there still people I need to reconnect with? Heal old wounds? You bet there are. Will I do my best to reach out to them before it's too late? You bet.

My hope is this book has inspired you to do the same.

Living each day without a sense of resentment or anger toward anyone, solving differences, and always making your friends feel like there is something in them gets you ready for whatever the day brings.

The last section in this book covered what I know best. Helping people "Protect Those They Love from Those They Owe." Having worked at the corporate level with a large life insurance company, to a rookie agent, to my own general agency, I have seen how lives can be impacted either positively or negatively with the unexpected death of a loved one. I want you to live each day with the knowledge that whether you live to age 100 or die tomorrow, those you love will still have the same life you wanted for them. It will help you sleep easier each night.

Read more in my book *Beating Taxes & Cheating Death,* available on Amazon.

This book started with the quote from Pastor Adrian Rogers, "You never truly learn to live until you are no longer afraid to die." For most of us, we will live a long time on this earth, and I wanted to show how you can live a full life with no fear of death. There are studies which predict that there will be over a million people in America and over 6 million worldwide over the age of 100 by the year 2050.

Go out and live your life with no fear, so at the end, whenever that is, you can say, "I am glad I did," not, "I wish I had."

Please send questions or comments to
PapaSoob@SoobEnt.com.

Chapter 13

THE AUTHOR
(Why should you want to
listen to me on these subjects?)

"Life should not be a journey to the grave with the intention of arriving safely in a pretty and well-preserved body, but rather to skid in broadside in a cloud of smoke, thoroughly used up, totally worn out, and loudly proclaiming "Wow! What a Ride!"
—**Hunter S. Thompson**, *The Proud Highway: Saga of a Desperate Southern Gentleman, 1955-1967*

The writing of this book has taken me a lot longer than I expected. In fact, there were several times I thought it was finished only to have another thought or story come to mind.

This is my third book, which is remarkable since I failed so many English classes in high school and college. I should have a master's in English by now. Even with spell check and other devices to help people like me, I am grateful to the many friends and family who reviewed and corrected this work.

This book comes from my heart and years of experience in the three areas the book covers: Spirituality, Relationships, and use of Life Insurance.

I consider myself a child of God, who strives to develop his character, conversation, and conduct to reflect His love in my life and in the lives that my life touches. There are days when this seems impossible, but it is the goal.

I am not a pastor, theologian, or reverend, so please seek out a pastor or Bible teaching scholar to verify what has been written. I have been blessed to have had the experience of being a part of different religious sects in Christianity.

You have read my testimony and journey in Chapter 3. Here is summary of what I said earlier and a few points I left out.

I was raised in the Holy Trinity Armenian Apostolic Church, attended Sunday School, was married, and served as Chairman of the Board of Trustees there. In my teens, I attended the First Methodist Church in Fresno where I was introduced to the person of Jesus Christ. In my adult life, I have attended Evangelical Free Church, Community-based Bible teaching churches, and different Charismatic churches. My most influential spiritual learning has come from an organization called the Christian Business Men's Connection (CBMC) here in Fresno. It was with this non-denominational organization that I learned to study the Bible through a program called "Operation Timothy." It is a 16-week course that took my leader, Tom Sommers, and me three years to complete.

Let me encourage you to take the time to read the Bible. There are several excellent translations that make it easy to read and understand. I once had a Catholic friend remark when she understood the difference between religion and a relationship, "I can't believe I based my faith on a book I never read." I was in that same situation until fifty-one. Please don't wait. Get into a Bible teaching Church. Read the entire Bible for yourself, and then make up your own mind. That's what I did.

My background, in the area of personal relationships, comes from my experience as Recreation Therapist at California State Mental Hospital, as the Chairman of the Fresno County Mental Health Association, as a member of the Fresno City & County Task Force on Alcoholism, and as Chairman of the Advisory Board for the San Francisco School of Psychology, Fresno campus. The advice given is not as a social worker, psychologist or psychiatrist, but as a person who has experienced 80 plus years of relationships—some good some not so good. I pulled from experiences of people who have had years working with people at the end of life.

The section on leaving a legacy and providing for those left behind comes from working in the life insurance profession since 1980. It is the one section that I have professional credentials to address. My uniqueness is that I have learned about the profession at all levels. I have the professional designation of Chartered Life Underwriter (CLU), and I have qualified for the Million Dollar Round Table, when in personal production.

I started as an agent in Mutual Company, working in a branch office for a major stock insurance company, owning my own general agency then spending nine years as a home office employee for the same major life insurance company.

More in-depth information on life insurance can be found in my book *Beating Taxes & Cheating Death: Insider Information on Life Insurance*. It is available on Amazon.com/books/arsenmarsooobian

The information in this section is not to be used as tax or legal advice. You are encouraged to seek your own counsel to determine the best way for you to provide for your own loved ones.

If you have the time and are moved to comment on this work, please contact me at: PapaSoob@SoobEnt.com. It would be a blessing to hear from you.

Section IV

ONE LAST WORD

NOTES:

If you have comments and or questions for the author use these pages to capture your thoughts while still fresh. Then if you would like to, pass them along to Arsen S. Marsoobian, AKA Papa Soob. PapaSoob@SoobEnt.com

NOTES

NOTES

NOTES

NOTES

NOTES

ACKNOWLEDGEMENTS

"It may take a village to raise a child, but it for sure takes a lot of loving friends to write a book."
—**Arsen S. Marsoobian**, author

Well, it took a village of friends and family to raise this book from the original thoughts to what you have in your hand. If you meet any of them, be sure to say thank you because they took a lot of their valuable time to read, reread and make invaluable suggestions and corrections.

A thank you from me is not nearly enough. I love each one of you, and I appreciate your love and support through this two-year process.

Robert Mano, speaker, consultant, executive coach and author of *Moving Beyond Your Limitations: Building a Business that Causes God to Smile.* He is also a brother in Christ, who guided me through all stages of this writing. He challenged what I was trying to say and made me uncomfortable at times. He helped me take it from just an idea to a finished product. I will always remember his timely suggestions whether it was a Bible verse or the order of the chapters. We did this early Friday mornings while sitting in his living room.

Ruth Klein, best-selling author of five books, professional speaker on branding and literary work, writing coach, is one of my best friends. Her reviews and insights to the stories, their meanings and relevance to the chapters were remarkable. Her honest evaluation of not understanding the value of some of the religious stories helped me write them in a clearer manner. Thank you for all the texts, emails, webinars, phone calls, and private sessions of encouragement to keep moving to get this message out. You truly are my "Jewish Princess."

Morgan Marsoobian, my granddaughter. Graduate 2016 from UC Santa Barbara, magna cum laude, in marketing, is now attending CSU Fresno to get California teaching credentials. Thank you, Morgan, for taking the time away from your studies to correct the grammar, formatting, and for moving the document over to Google Docs to make it easier to rewrite. Your comments on the dedication to Grandma Rosellen, along with your sister Taylor's, were most helpful.

Taylor Marsoobian, my granddaughter, graduated in communications from UC Santa Barbara. A big help in reading and commenting on the dedication section and early drafts of the manuscript. Also appreciate her help and support in marketing strategies in getting word out.

Eric Hughes, author, business owner, marketing director, for his help in writing press releases, reviews of book as it moved along for two years. His taking time to meet me for coffee to talk strategy in marketing and stories to either include or exclude.

Chris Terrence, author, television personality, sports announcer and friend for over fifty years. His early comments and review of the book helped form the structure and flow of the chapters.

The suggestions and editing of the following friends added much to the final version. Richard Smith, author, business executive; and a few who wanted to remain anonymous, and to the many in my internet family who promoted the book to their contacts.

To Michelle Prince and her staff for all the professional help in editing and getting this in readable form for you.

Love and blessings to you all,
Arsen S. Marsoobian, aka Papa SOOB

BIBLIOGRAPHY

THE HOLY BIBLE, NEW INTERNATIONAL VERSION,
LIFE APPLICATION STUDY BIBLE, COPYRIGHT BY
TYNDALE HOUSE PUBLISHERS, INC, 1988-1989
1990-1991-2005. PUBLISHED BY ZONDERVAN

Don't Die: 3 Essential Truths For Your Fulfilled and Happy Life.
Copyright 2012, Author Arsen S. Marsoobian. Published
by SOOB Enterprises, Fresno CA.

Heaven. Copyright 2004. Author Randy Alcorn. Eternal
Perspective Ministries. Published by Tyndale House
Publishing,

*How To Know God: The Soul's Journey into the Mystery of
Mysteries.* Copyright 2000. Author Deepak Chopra, M.D..
Published by Harmony Books Member of the Crown
Publishing Group

No Wonder They Call Him The Savior. Copyright 1986. Author
Max Lucado. Published by Mulmomah Press part of
Questar publishing Family

The Case For Faith. Copyright 2000. Author Lee Strobel.
Published by Zondervan

The Case For Christianity: Answer Book. Copyright 2014.
Author Lee Strobel. Published by Zondervan

Morgan James
Speakers Group

We connect Morgan James published authors with live and online events and audiences who will benefit from their expertise.

 Morgan James makes all of our titles available
through the Library for All Charity Organization.

www.LibraryForAll.org